BUILDING A WINNING CULTURE IN GOVERNMENT

A BLUEPRINT FOR DELIVERING SUCCESS IN THE PUBLIC SECTOR

PATRICK R. LEDDIN, PHD

SHAWN D. MOON

For information about special discounts for bulk purchases, please contact government@franklincovey.com.

Building a Winning Culture in Government: A Blueprint for Delivering Success in the Public Sector

ISBN: (p) 978-1-63353-764-4
BISAC POL030000 POLITICAL SCIENCE / American Government / National

Printed in the United States of America

TABLE OF CONTENTS

CHAPTER 4 — 56

The Operating System That Builds Effective Leaders at Every Level

CHAPTER 5 — 97

Practice 1: Lead With Purpose

INTRODUCTION

Peter Drucker famously said, "Culture eats strategy for breakfast." In doing so, he identified a phenomenon that leaders have struggled with throughout history: *It is one thing to have a great strategy, but it's quite another to accomplish it.* Never has this statement been more true—or more challenging—than for today's government organizations.

Whether operating at the federal, state, or local level, government organizations face increased media scrutiny, reduced funding, and the many challenges of moving large, multi-layered, and highly regulated organizations. It's no surprise that many government organizations report that their employees are less engaged than ever and that leaders feel helpless to change the situation.

In many cases, employees and leaders are caught in a vicious cycle. Performance declines, scrutiny increases, and employee paralysis ensues. Repeat.

How do you break this cycle?

You change the mindset from "leaders are a select few in the organization" to "everyone can and should be a leader." This simple, yet significant shift is key to creating an effective government organization in the twenty-first century. If every member of the organization is leading from where they are, it also allows government organizations to leverage the power of five highly effective practices:

1. Find the voice of the organization and connect and align accordingly (a.k.a. lead with purpose).
2. Execute your strategy with excellence.
3. Unleash and engage people to do infinitely more than they imagined they could.
4. Be the most trusted organization possible.
5. Create fervent loyalty with all stakeholders.

For years, FranklinCovey has helped government organizations employ these practices, develop leaders at every level, create results, and ignite their ultimate mission essential—a winning culture. We have worked with thousands of teams and hundreds of organizations at every level of government. Now we want to help you drive mission success by creating a winning culture of your own.

In this book we discuss the challenge and opportunity associated with building a powerful, winning culture within government and frame the paradigm of "leadership at all levels." We review in some depth the five practices you need to create this culture.

Leaders are a significant leverage point for any team or organization. What the leaders say and how they behave represent an organization's single largest opportunity for affecting change. Perhaps you are a leader with responsibility for a team, agency, or division, or perhaps you don't have any formal direct reports. Either way, you can be a force for change, for creating engagement, and—ultimately—for getting the most important things done.

The great cultural anthropologist Margaret Mead once said, "Never doubt that a small group of thoughtful, committed citizens can change the world; indeed, it's the only thing that ever has."

Our goal with this book is not to help you change the world. It is to help you create lasting change within your own circles of influence with the knowledge that your influence can grow over time to become truly significant. Our goal with this book is to help you change *your* world. We invite you to begin the journey.

CHAPTER 1

AN INCREASINGLY PRESSURIZED ENVIRONMENT

THE CHALLENGE OF OPERATING IN A CONSTANTLY CHANGING SYSTEM

-

"All organizations are perfectly designed to get the results they get."
–Arthur W. Jones

-

As keynote speaker, Patrick was biding his time until his turn at the podium and watching the current presenter. The organization's executive director was about ten minutes into her remarks, and the audience was engaged. Not a passive *she's the boss so we have to listen* type of engagement; they were genuinely enthralled by her presentation.

Her message aligned around a single theme: *the organization needed to better meet the evolving needs of its customers*. Although the organization had a stellar track record and an untarnished reputation, the leaders in the room needed to deliver higher-quality services on time, every time, and at the lowest cost possible. Theirs was a competitive environment, and if they didn't raise their performance, someone else would subvert their efforts.

In our work with clients, we've heard many similar presentations in many other conference rooms. The leader was dynamic, the argument was sound, and the strategy was clear. However, this wasn't a multinational corporation or a mid-size enterprise trying to reach the next level. The leader who mesmerized her audience was in charge of a government agency.

Her insights were spot-on. She understood that they were living in a world of diminishing resources, increasing scrutiny, and uncompromising demands. She had figured out that the organization was operating in an increasingly pressurized environment, and she was passionately conveying that message so that all in attendance would see and ultimately respond to the emerging environment by thinking and acting more effectively.

The executive director explained that if they did not continue to improve, they would fall prey to a growing number of threats both within the larger government structure (internal) and outside of the government (external). From an internal perspective, other government organizations were competing with them for funding, technology, facilities, and personnel. Although these internal competitors had existed to varying degrees for years, the acceleration level was tremendous. In fact, these competitors were not competing simply for an extra employee or some additional funding; they were trying to take over her organization's very mission. The other organizations were trying to consume them.

Simultaneously, the external environment was riddled with pitfalls. Contractors were absorbing roles that had once been considered inherently government and off-limits to outsourcing. A wide range of stakeholders—including legislators, businesses, and everyday citizens—were actively questioning and intervening in daily operations. Fueled by a 24/7 news cycle, a staggering number of cable channels, and the ubiquitous nature of the Internet, these stakeholders insisted every mistake signaled an epidemic and required sweeping changes, and that shared mission signified redundancy that needed to be wiped out. Add to these realities increased security as a result of terrorism, a less than desirable job market, and a recovering economy. The organization had never faced an environment like this before. The executive director wanted each of her 300 managers to understand that in today's world, poor customer service in one part of the organization or a scandal in another could threaten the job of everyone in the room.

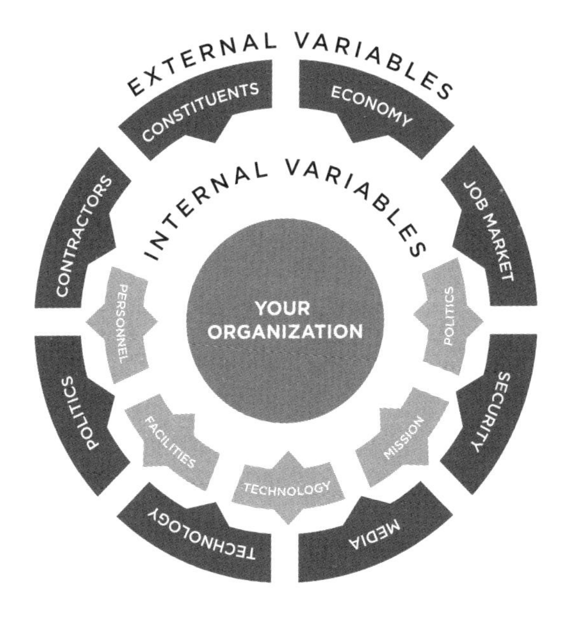

Of course, the concepts of competition, increased scrutiny, and growing pressure are not new to the public sector. Consider these examples:

- A charity focused on finding a cure for cancer is not the only organization with the mission of tackling this serious health condition. In the United States, the American Cancer Society deals with different cancer types; however, separate organizations tackle specific forms of this disease such as pancreatic cancer, liver cancer, breast cancer, and children's cancer, just to name a few. The market has been segmented, and organizations are tailoring their messages and approaches. Whether acknowledged or not, these organizations—all with a just and important mission—are pitted against each other. Potential donor pockets are only so deep. These groups must be creative, compelling, and relentless to get people's attention and garner a slice of the market.

- A museum realizes that it is not the only game in town. Other museums are trying to attract the attention of the same patrons and visitors. Perhaps each organization has historically filled its own niche; maybe they even worked together as part of the community. However, as the environment becomes pressurized, each creeps into the other's space. When a major traveling exhibit comes to town, museums that serve children, science buffs, historians, and art lovers all compete for the same exhibition.
- The United States Postal Service (USPS) has dealt with the pressure of FedEx and United Parcel Service (UPS) for years. A growing reliance on email and the cost of operations and employee benefits for USPS as a large federal agency exacerbate the situation. As a result, the USPS posted a loss of $25.9 billion in a three-year period (2011–2013), while experiencing a 5.9 percent decrease in mail volume.[1] These numbers suggest an erosion of USPS business, but there is more to the story. Beginning FY (Fiscal Year) 2014, USPS

1. United States Postal Service. "2013 Report to Congress." https://about.usps.com/publications/annual-report-comprehensive-statement-2013/annualreport2013_002.htm#ep998349

> marketing initiatives are driving e-commerce growth and efforts to modernize operations are underway to improve delivery effectiveness.

You might be thinking, *But those governments and nonprofits operate more like businesses. My organization is different. We don't have FedEx breathing down our necks. We fill a vital role that is inherently government and something no one else can do. There is no competition; we are the only game in town.*

We invite you to think again.

Consider the city of Sandy Springs, Georgia. Located fifteen miles north of Atlanta, Sandy Springs is a community of approximately 100,000 residents. Like similar cities, Sandy Springs provides a wide range of services to its constituents. Unlike most cities, the vast majority of Sandy Springs' work is outsourced to private contractors. The entire town has only *seven* government employees, and the whole Sandy Springs operation "is housed in a generic, one-story industrial park...the people you meet here work for private companies through a variety of contracts."[2]

If you apply for a business license in Sandy Springs, want to make a structural change to your home, or need assistance with trash collection, you will work with contractors in Boston, San Francisco, and across the "pond" in Coventry,

2. Segal, David. "A Georgia Town Takes the People's Business Private." June 23, 2012. *The New York Times*. http://www.nytimes.com/2012/06/24/business/a-georgia-town-takes-the-peoples-business-private.html.

England. Think this is a one-off experiment that won't extend to your organization? Consider that the city has no long-term debt and no fleet of vehicles to maintain. While cities like Detroit and Chicago grapple with significant challenges, the first city manager of Sandy Springs, Oliver Porter, met with government leaders in Japan, Iceland, Britain, and the country of Georgia to share the Sandy Springs story. Meanwhile, the current city manager, John McDonough, is producing annual reports with the look and feel of private industry, showing an eight-year winning record and articulating a vision for the future.

Whether you work for local, state, or federal government, volunteer at or run a nonprofit, serve on the board of a charitable hospital, or work in any part of the public sector, competition is present, growing, and intensifying. Yours is a world of competition.

We're not saying, "Act like a business." As Jim Collins wrote, "We must reject the idea—well-intentioned, but dead wrong—that the primary path to greatness in the social sector is to become 'more like a business.' Most businesses—like most of anything else in life—fall somewhere between mediocre and good."[3] Moreover, your organization's purpose and the measures of success may be very different from those of most businesses. In your world, it is likely that mission

3. Jim Cowllins. *Good to Great and the Social Sectors: A Monograph to Accompany Good to Great*. HarperCollins, 2005, 1.

is more important than market share, and service trumps profits. Additionally the inherent challenges of enforcing laws, implementing policies, and ensuring public safety or national security rarely correlate with stellar customer-service numbers—after all, the very nature of your work may cause you and your people to say no. For the most part, customers don't like that word. Throw into the mix the public sector's unique constraints associated with hiring, positioning, developing, rewarding, promoting, and—at times—terminating employees, and the concept of acting like a business becomes not just difficult but downright naïve to suggest.

We are saying that to be a truly great public-sector organization, you must recognize the pressures that surround you and proactively rise to the challenge. You must see the world as the executive director in our example saw it and put a system in place to ensure success both today and tomorrow as the pressures in the competitive cauldron become more and more intense. This book is a road map for such an operating system.

CHAPTER 2

THE PARADIGM: LEADERSHIP IS A CHOICE, NOT JUST A POSITION

A NEW PARADIGM: EVERYONE ON YOUR TEAM SHOULD BE A LEADER—AND IT IS YOUR JOB TO GET THEM THERE

-

"Leadership is a team sport, and teams require collective leadership."
–Dave Ulrich

-

It Starts With Culture

Think of a top-notch organization you know—one you wholeheartedly tell others to work for, or whose story you share with friends at dinner. Why do you recommend it? What makes it so unique? Or, to put it more forcefully, why is that organization so remarkable, and rare, that you tell stories about it? What causes you to feel so strongly about the organization?

After thirty-plus years of partnering with some of the greatest public- and private-sector organizations and leaders worldwide, we know that top organizations share the most powerful, hard-to-replicate, and sustainable competitive advantage: a winning culture.

We define culture as the collective behavior of your people—what the majority of your people do the majority of the time; the nature of the language and relationships; and the spoken and unspoken values, norms, and systems at work. Winning cultures are filled with superb people who deliver as promised time after time. In the public sector, a wining culture means that customers go to you not just because they must, but because they know you can effectively provide services or support. They give them someone and something to trust. Winning cultures are unique, deliberately designed and maintained, and rare.

DEFINITION:

culture: *the collective behavior of your people—what the majority of your people do the majority of the time; the nature of the language and relationships within the culture; and the spoken and unspoken values, norms, and systems at work.*

"Winning cultures are filled with superb people who deliver as promised time after time."

Culture That Stays on Track

In the 1830s, Charles Pearson proposed a rather ingenious, and arguably mad, idea for public transportation. Some fourteen years later, a tunnel began to weave its way under the streets of London. Nine years after that, the first segment of what would become London's Underground opened for business. Although the system's original visionary, Charles Pearson, was no longer alive to make the journey, some 30,000 Londoners climbed aboard the Metropolitan Line during its first day of operation.

"Winning cultures are unique, deliberately designed and maintained, and rare."

Since its opening day in 1863, the Underground has grown to 11 lines, 249 miles of track, and some 270 stations. Transportation for London (TfL) operates the "Tube," as it has come to be called, and in 2014, it carried a record 1.26

billion travelers, marking an increase of over 33 percent in the last decade.

Keeping pace with the rapid growth of both the city population and passenger numbers is a significant challenge for TfL. Imagine trying to renovate stations, replace aging trains, build new control centers, and upgrade network signals while transporting four million people. One leader said that modernizing the Tube is similar to "doing open-heart surgery whilst the patient is playing tennis." Those of you in the Washington, D.C., metro area during the update in 2017 can likely relate.

So how does an organization accomplish such a mammoth task without disrupting commuters and frustrating thousands of employees? TfL decided that the answer resided in its ability to build leadership capacity and establish core values. In other words, they needed to deliberately develop a *culture* that would meet the demands of their ever-expanding mission.

In 2006, TfL began training managers on the organization's core behaviors of accountability, fairness, consistency, collaboration, and directness. After two years, the general manager of TfL's Bakerloo Line, Lance Ramsay, believed that to truly achieve the culture he envisioned, he needed to empower his organization's team members as well.

Ramsay, a TfL employee since 1983, knew how things operated in the Underground. The Tube's history was heavily influenced by the military and its command-and-control culture. Ramsay determined that his 800 Bakerloo Line team members would benefit from FranklinCovey's proven process of behavior change. FranklinCovey began by training Ramsay's leadership team in *The 7 Habits of Highly Effective People*™ and certifying internal Bakerloo Line facilitators and champions at all levels of Ramsay's organization.

Just as an individual's character is tested in crisis, an organization's culture is exposed under intense pressure. The Bakerloo Line was tested from 2008 to 2013 as it experienced rapid growth coupled with major events ranging from the 2012 Summer Olympics to the marriage of Prince William and Kate Middleton. Throughout this period, the Bakerloo Line not only kept up with the demands of continuous system improvements and unprecedented growth in passenger numbers, but they increased their performance:

- Passenger wait times dropped by 37 percent.
- On-time schedule operation increased from 94 percent in 2008 to 97.8 percent in 2012.
- Delays over fifteen minutes declined by 61 percent.
- Customer satisfaction improved to an 83 out of 100.

Beyond the metrics, Bakerloo Line team members said that the culture change has improved union negotiations, senior-leadership communication, and accountability throughout the organization. As manager Dave Proffitt said, "I think we've almost grown together, and we are far more open… there is a very high degree of trust within the room. We've all done it together, and have been mutually supportive."

That feeling of mutual support, cooperation, and leadership at all organizational levels has become the Bakerloo Line culture. Ramsay knows that the efforts of his team to deliberately develop a winning culture is key to keeping their organization on track as the turnstiles turn more frequently and train capacity continues to soar.

A Culture That Is Derailed With Bad Leadership

Let's look at a different kind of culture and the behaviors, language, and results it can produce.

Jan and her sister were in the garden enjoying a cup of coffee, when her sister's husband, Tom, joined them. As he sat down, he glanced at his phone. "One year, three months, two days, six hours, four minutes, and exactly thirty seconds until I retire."

"What are you talking about?" Jan asked. Tom was bright, capable, and had years of great work ahead of him. Or so she thought.

"I've got an app on my phone that counts down to the moment I retire."

Jan thought this must be a joke. "You're not going to retire, Tom," she said. "With your background, your organization will hire you back as a consultant—and pay you five times as much."

"No," Tom said. "You don't get it. When the countdown ends, I can retire with all my benefits. I'm not working for that organization one second more."

"Why not?"

"My organization used to be a great place to work," Tom said. "I loved everything about it; but two years ago, things really changed. We got a new boss, and he told us how things were going to be from now on. Some of us had been around for a few years, so we asked, 'Do we have any say in this?' I also remarked, 'We have appreciated the loyalty we have felt from the organization over the years. Should we continue to expect that?' And he gave us a look—let's just say it's a look I've gotten familiar with. The new boss then said, rather curtly, 'If you want loyalty, get a dog.' "

When was Tom's true retirement date? Despite what his phone said, he hung it up two years ago. That's when he stopped doing his best work, when he ceased being fully engaged. He's been physically on the job, he does what's expected, but nothing more. Tom could have given many more years—perhaps his finest years—but the organization that used to engage his body, mind, spirit, and passion will not benefit from his contribution.

He will give his best to something else.

Could there be a stronger contrast in cultures between the ineffective organization Tom has "retired" from and the highly effective team at the Bakerloo Line?

The Challenge of Human Capital

Four blocks from the White House in Washington, D.C., an Art Deco office stands at the intersection of New York Avenue and 12th Street NW. The majority of the building's second floor is home to the Partnership for Public Service (PPS). Over a decade ago, Samuel J. Heyman founded this nonprofit, nonpartisan organization to revitalize the United States federal government by transforming how the government works. He wanted to inspire a new generation of people to public service, similar to how John F. Kennedy had inspired him some forty years earlier.

Each year, PPS, with assistance from the global management-consulting firms Deloitte Consulting LLP and Hay Group, compiles and analyzes the *Best Places to Work in the Federal Government* rankings. The rankings draw from the Office of Personnel Management's Federal Employee Viewpoint Survey and provide specific information about employee satisfaction and commitment.

In May 2014, PPS President and CEO Max Stier presented his assessment to the U.S. Senate Committee on Homeland Security and Governmental Affairs Subcommittee on Efficiency and Effectiveness of Federal Programs and the Federal Workforce. Stiers' comments expressed several causes for concern. "Government-wide, federal employee job satisfaction and commitment dropped for the third year in a row, tumbling three points to a score of 57.8 on a scale of 100. This represents the lowest overall *Best Places to Work* score since the rankings were first launched in 2003." Stier contrasted the level of satisfaction and commitment of federal workers to those in the private sector, which improved 0.7 points in 2013 to 70.7, according to the Hay Group. Stier's testimony provided a litany of issues that impact the development of the federal workforce, including effective leadership, compensation, and performance-management processes, and provided legislative recommendations for Congress focused on the government's human capital.[4]

Human capital.

4. Max, Stier. Written Testimony to the Senate Committee on Homeland Security and Government Affairs Subcommittee on Efficiency and Effectiveness of Federal Programs and the Federal Workforce. "A More Efficient and Effective Government: Cultivating the Federal Workforce." May 6, 2014.

What does that mean? *Human* capital? Don't they mean *financial* capital? Isn't it *financial capital* that organizations are concerned about? Why are they worried about human capital? Why is that a top-of-mind issue?

Let's tackle the financial-capital question first. There is no doubt that finances matter: a vision without the necessary resources to make it happen is just a hallucination. However, as necessary as funding is, it is equally insufficient. Throwing money at a problem doesn't guarantee a successful outcome, nor does trying to operate like a business guarantee a government organization's success. Jim Collins said it well: "For a social sector organization, however, performance must be assessed relative to mission, not financial returns. In the social sectors, the critical question is not 'How much money do we make per dollar of invested capital?' but 'How effectively do we deliver on our mission and make a distinctive impact, relative to our resources?' "

We have found that public-sector leaders across North America, Asia, Europe, and all corners of the world agree that their top priority is developing employees with the skills, knowledge, and experience to create tremendous value for the organization, its mission, and those it serves—in other words, developing human capital. They know about the dramatic difference between team members on the Bakerloo Line team and employees like Tom. The ultimate mission essential in the public sector belongs to organizations that can get the best contribution possible from the best people they can find. In simple terms, it means inspiring and motivating people to bring the best they can give, to the point where they fight through rush hour on the Bakerloo Line for you![5]

It raises the question, "Why is there no outbreak of great cultures in the public sector if so many leaders and employees are aware of both the problem and the opportunity?"

Let's explore one of the problems: *The majority of government workers in the United States are not engaged or are actively disengaged from their work.* According to Gallup, it's 71 percent. That means leaders have *failed* to motivate and inspire more than 7 out of 10 of their workers. Consider this: In the United States government alone, there are 2.7 million civilian workers. That means that nearly 2 million of them are not engaged in their work.[6]

"The majority of the United States government workers are not engaged or are actively disengaged from their work."

---

5. Franklin Covey Co. "Catalysing Change on the Bakerloo Line: The 7 Habits at Work Underground in London." October 2011. http://franklincoveyresearch.org/catalog/Transport_for_London.pdf.

6. *State of the Global Workplace: Employee Engagement Insights for Business Leaders Worldwide*, The Gallup Organization, 2013. http://www.gallup.com/strategicconsulting/164735/state-global-workplace.aspx

Imagine extrapolating this number to include public-sector workers at all levels of the government (federal, state, and local) and not-for-profit organizations in countries around the world. Even a conservative figure suggests millions of people like Tom—each one unique, with talent, skill, and passion, and great contributions to make—are mentally and emotionally retired.

When Dr. Stephen R. Covey spoke to his audiences around the globe, he would always ask, "How many of you honestly believe that the vast majority of the people in your organization possess more intelligence, talent, capability, creativity, and resourcefulness than their present jobs require or even allow?" In every case, nearly every hand went up.

"How many of you honestly believe that the vast majority of the people in your organization possess more intelligence, talent, capability, creativity, and resourcefulness than their present jobs require or even allow?"

—Stephen R. Covey

Why is this so? Because too many leaders don't know *how* to engage people. When leaders don't know exactly how to do something, they can default to the things they do know how to do—budget, project management, operations, etc. Oftentimes in a highly regulated environment, these are also the things that are most constrained and, ultimately, especially in the case of budget, not in a leader's Circle of Influence®. A leader's job is to establish an operating system that allows people to contribute their very best, consistently and compellingly. And because intentionally building and maintaining a winning culture is completely within a leader's Circle of Influence, this is also his or her most powerful lever for achieving results.

The Government Executive Media Group explains that the research conducted by Gallup, along with the results of the PPS *Best Places to Work* rankings, clearly show that leaders play a key role in growing employee engagement, empowerment, and appreciation. Unfortunately, Government Executive also reports that empowerment ranks an abysmal 43.8 out of 100 among government leaders. Some cast the issue aside, arguing that the low score is a function of the unique challenges to government organizations, which include pay, policies, and systems. There is some truth to this claim. The systems can be very challenging at times; you can't just show a poor performer the door. Others suggest that the score is the result of the growing competitive cauldron in the public sector—outside pressures, diminishing resources, and increased scrutiny.

True, some of these leadership challenges are unique to the idiosyncrasies of the public sector. Engaging people is a tough job in the public sector, but it's a challenge in the private sector as well. According to a survey on global CEO performance by Stanford University's Center for Leadership Development and Research, engaging people is rated the "top weakness" of CEOs. Some leaders, like Tom's boss, actively discourage people. Mostly, though, they just don't have the skill to lead people. After reviewing the Stanford study, *Forbes Magazine* concluded that "CEOs are doing a lousy job when it comes to people management."[7]

Leaders know they're not doing a good job managing their people, and it troubles them. They need to capture the hearts and minds of their people to build a team like TfL's Bakerloo Line. It's the biggest job they have, but they don't know how to do it. And it's not just a senior leader's problem; leaders at all levels struggle with it, particularly those who are new in their supervisory roles.

Let's face it, there is no outbreak of winning cultures in the public sector. While culture makes all the difference, too many organizations leave building their culture to chance. We're reminded of the quote by acclaimed management

---

7. David F. Larcker, Stephen Miles, Brian Tayan, and Michelle E. Gutman, "2013 CEO Performance Evaluation Survey." Stanford University Center for Leadership Development and Research. https://www.gsb.stanford.edu/faculty-research/publications/2013-ceo-performance-evaluation-survey (May 2013).

expert Peter Drucker: "Culture eats strategy for breakfast." Understanding this is key to creating a successful organization.

Being Deliberate in Building Culture

How much time and energy do we devote to strategic plans and initiatives, metrics, goals, and project planning? Look around your office. Do you have posters announcing goals, email signature blocks attesting to the newest initiative, and strategic plans with your organization's acronym emblazoned across the cover?

But have you ever forgotten to address culture during a key strategic shift? Ever experienced a culture pushing back on a strategy or a change-management initiative? We recall hearing a long-term devoted public servant speaking to her team in the hallway after a new political leader's election and inspiring "call to action" speech. She said, "Be respectful, and know that we can wait out any of this leader's strategies…we've done it before and we can do it again." That's culture pushing back. People cross their arms with the intent of waiting things out—and the "meeting after the meeting" undermines all of your well-intended efforts.

A great culture must be leader-led, designed intentionally, and have an established framework of behaviors and language that aligns the performance of everyone in the organization. Everyone must know how to win and fully understand the why behind the what. It is not enough to simply state the path forward; a great leader must deliberately invite every person into that way forward. Everyone must lead. Can you imagine if everyone in your organization behaved like a leader? What results could you achieve?

A great culture must be leader-led, designed intentionally, and have an established framework of behaviors and language that aligns the performance of everyone in the organization.

That's the reason for this book. The Ultimate Mission Essential for public-sector organizations is the paradigm that everyone on your team should be a leader. Too many see leadership as a title. But leadership is a choice, not just a position. This doesn't mean the organizational chart is thrown out the window; it simply means all people take ownership of ensuring success.

Leadership is a choice, not just a position.

The first step is adopting the mindset that everyone on your team can lead. It's your job to make them leaders and to inspire them to embrace their roles. This happens by establishing a framework (or an operating system, which we'll discuss in Chapter 4) for getting the job done effectively. This framework should be ubiquitous and not role-specific. It demands that leaders "show up" and model the culture, rather than talk about it in generic terms (or worse yet, "talk at" team members about it). It will develop high-character and high-competence leaders at every level of the organization. It will give everyone a common language and a set of behaviors they can depend on as they work to achieve results year after year.

The People Behind the Activities

You and your people are your organization's only sustainable competitive advantage. No matter which segment of the public sector you work in, when the people quit work for the night, your competitive advantage quits too. The brains of a contributor like Tom can shut down anytime, even during work hours. You might say, "What about our mission? organizational structure? internal rewards program? work processes? computer systems? Aren't they advantages that will overcome the public sector's growing competitive cauldron?"

Obviously, competitive advantages can come from many sources, but the bottom line is that none of those advantages exist apart from what people actually *do*. Your mission, your structure, your rewards programs—whatever your resources and capabilities—are all the product of people working together. If *they* don't work well, your advantage is gone.

An organization can have a number of unique aspects, but if people don't do the things needed to leverage them, sustain them, and live up to them, they will evaporate. Your organization may have well-refined processes, but if your people couldn't care less about maintaining them, the whole thing is a house of cards. *The behavior of your people is the ultimate source of your competitive advantage.*

No matter what you think your competitive advantage is, *people* create it, sustain it, leverage it, and make it work. If they are as engaged as the people of the Bakerloo Line, they will pull the organization forward if they have to. But if they are like Tom—unexcited about the organization, uncaring, indifferent, even alienated from it—your competitive advantage will disappear. If they are not giving their best efforts to your strategy, you can forget the dazzling wording of your mission or the compelling reason the organization exists. If there are enough Toms on your team—and the evidence shows there are many Toms, despite what you may think and no matter how they smile at you as you pass—no matter how many times they nod their head in seeming agreement with your goal, your competitive advantage is over.

The sum of what everyone does every day is called "culture." It is what the majority of the people do the majority of the time. It's a reflection of an organization's collective behaviors, the language and behaviors of its people, and the spoken and unspoken values, norms, and systems that exist. Another way to frame the top-of-mind issue in the Partnership for Public Sector's efforts is, "How do I build a winning culture?" Clearly, it's a crucial question: Dr. Stephen R. Covey once said,

> "The only sustainable competitive advantage that will long endure is the core competency of a high-trust[8], principle-centered organizational culture of committed people aligned to a common vision. Your competitors will copy your marketing, your product, your systems, your structure, your strategy, but they cannot duplicate the unique advantage of the trust, *esprit de corps*, and performance of your people."

The leader's main job is to build that kind of culture, and it is the behavior of the leader that determines the culture. Author and world-renowned business coach Ram Charan said, "The culture of any organization is simply the collective

8. More will be said about how to establish a high-trust culture in Chapter 8.

behavior of its leaders. If you want to change your culture, change the collective behavior of your leaders.

Culture is the reason a Bakerloo Line worker keeps things on track and gets the job done. Culture is the reason a nurse stops a medical procedure if she spots a quality problem. Culture is the reason military-aviation ground crews run to meet an arriving plane. Culture is the reason a nonprofit leader travels halfway around the world to meet with volunteers supporting the organization's cause. These are the behaviors of highly engaged people in a high-trust culture: it's just what they do.

But culture is also the reason a great potential contributor like Tom comes to work every day, smiles and nods, and contributes nothing.

According to Harvard professor Clayton Christensen, "It is common to describe culture as the visible elements of a working environment: casual Fridays, free sodas in the cafeteria, or whether you can bring your dog to the office.... Those things don't define a culture. They're just artifacts of it."[9] Culture is much deeper. It is the habitual, instinctive behaviors of people. They are rooted in the character of people.

---

9. Clayton Christensen, James Allworth and Karen Dillon, *How Will You Measure Your Life?* HarperBusiness, 2012, 160.

That's why to gain the mission essential that counts most—a great culture—you need to go deep. Human behavior is the product of human character and mindset. It's the product of *paradigms*—the ways people see themselves and the world around them. To change the culture, you have to change people's paradigms.

Here's a simple example of what we mean by a paradigm that drives behavior. Shawn tells this story: "When my wife and I were newly married, we shared one car. She would drop me off at school in the morning before going to her job several miles in the other direction. Then she would drive back at noon to take me to my afternoon job and return to hers. At the end of the day, she would circle back and we would go home together. We put a lot of miles on our car that semester.

"One day, I needed to be at school early and had a lot of pressing projects at work in the afternoon, so we went carefully over the schedule that morning. I had no margin for error, so when I stepped into the parking lot, I knew she'd be there this time. She wasn't—and my temperature rose. I waited and waited and waited. I worried that maybe something had happened to her. A crisis at work? But after an hour, I determined that if nothing *had* happened, something *would* happen once she finally showed up!

"Then, after two hours and fifteen minutes of pacing and fretting and fuming—a stunning insight! *I had driven the car myself that day!* My wife was waiting for *me*! I gulped hard, trying to think of something to say to her.

"We both chuckle about it now. The point is, I had perceived the situation in a way that didn't fit with reality, and when my paradigm suddenly shifted, my behavior shifted too. I went from fuming and snarling to groveling and whimpering. That's the power of a Paradigm Shift."

Patrick shares a story about a public-sector leader who practiced a "kiss up, kick down" mentality. He said "yes" to everything his boss said without clarifying expectations and then would force his people to work on projects everyone knew were going nowhere. He had competent, capable people reporting to him, but he wasted their energy rewriting sentences on documents no one would read and building presentations no one would see. His unwillingness to ensure that he knew the desired outcomes of an effort caused his people to stop contributing. They stopped thinking; stopped acting without his specific direction. He had disengaged once-amazing contributors and had no idea his view of things was his downfall.

Paradigms drive practices. For example, if you're part of a culture that believes in the value of activity over results, you'll probably spend hours in conference rooms talking about all the work you are doing, but little about the outcomes you actually accomplished. In the end, a paradigm based on a false principle will fail you. Your practices or behaviors will bring *you* down.

Paradigms drive practices.

Clayton Christensen said, "A culture can be built consciously or evolve inadvertently."[10] Which do you prefer for your team or organization? You can consciously build a culture like the Bakerloo Line, or you can let it devolve into a disengaged team of Toms.

Is your organizational culture working for you or against you? We are inviting you to design your culture deliberately.

How to Effectively Change Behaviors

In many public-sector organizations, the typical approach to changing people's behavior is to reward or threaten them. This is what Stephen R. Covey called "the great jackass theory of human motivation—carrot and stick." The problem with this approach is that it treats people like animals, and it works only on the surface and only temporarily. Like Tom, people who are threatened develop a paradigm of fear, so

10. Christensen, *How Will You Measure Your Life*, 166.

they act out of fear. They will "work" for an organization, but they will never give their heart. They will never speak honestly, contribute freely, or do more than required. They will never, ever tell you what they really think.

They will be motivated all right (motivated to evade responsibility), but they will never be inspired. In today's workplace, many workers are afraid, and they act like it. They take little initiative, they avoid responsibility, they keep their thoughts to themselves—they bring as little as possible to the table so they won't get in trouble. This is the legacy of the Industrial Age. You will never capture people's hearts by treating them like jackasses, but that's how most managers lead.

You will never capture people's hearts by treating them like jackasses, but that's how most managers lead.

The secret to changing behavior is to change paradigms and enact highly effective practices built upon these new ways of thinking. That's the purpose of this book: to replace unproductive paradigms with inspiring new paradigms and corresponding practices that will unleash new and extraordinarily productive behavior. *That's the job you must do now.*

That's the purpose of this book: to replace unproductive paradigms with inspiring new paradigms and corresponding practices that will unleash new and extraordinarily productive behavior.

The story of the Bakerloo Line proves that this job, while challenging, can be done and that the results are dramatic. We helped this world leader in the Underground commuter transportation reach that ultimate competitive position in the public-sector level, and we can help you too.

Five Key Practices to Success

The common ways of thinking are often reactive and counterproductive. Consider. What kind of leader would you be if…

- No one but you felt a sense of responsibility for results?
- You didn't understand the combined power of your team?
- You failed to execute your most important goals?
- You didn't fully leverage the genius, talent, and skill of your team?

- There was a lack of trust in you, each other, or the organization?
- Your internal and external customers had no clear idea what kind of value you brought to them?
- There was little loyalty on your team to you, each other, or the organization?

FranklinCovey has over three decades of experience with hundreds of thousands of people in international organizations, small schools, and whole departments of government. They come to us to become highly effective organizations. We have five practices that show them how to do this, but it always begins with changed mindsets—paradigms—that will enable them to thrive. We have shown in this chapter that the first shift is seeing that your people are your ultimate competitive advantage and that you must engage them before you can successfully move forward. To do this, it is not your job to simply be the leader, but to make everyone a leader. Once this shift has occurred, it is time for you to shift your thinking in five key areas:

Common Practices	Highly Effective Practices
Create and post the mission statement in all public areas.	1. Find the Voice of the organization and connect and align accordingly (a.k.a. Lead With Purpose).
Develop a great strategy.	2. Execute your strategy with excellence.
Do more with less.	3. Unleash and engage people to do infinitely more than you imagined they could.
Become the provider/ employer of choice in your industry.	4. Be the most trusted provider/employer in your sector.
Satisfy customers.	5. Create fervent loyalty with customers.

Why these five practices? Each one is based on fundamental principles that never change. The principles of proactivity, execution, productivity, and trust underlie every great achievement: nothing has ever been accomplished in human history without them. People who live by the opposite values—reactivity, aimless activity, waste, mistrust—contribute little to the success of the organization. Similarly, the principles of mutual benefit and loyalty underlie every successful relationship. People who live by the opposite values—indifference to others and disloyalty—create no goodwill and work against the organization. The common ways of thinking are often reactive and counterproductive. We need this new model.

You can see for yourself why these Paradigm Shifts and new practices are vital. You can come up with many other success factors, but these five are inviolable. Leaders *must* be able to (1) find the "voice" of the organization, (2) execute with excellence, (3) unleash the productivity of people, (4) inspire trust, and (5) engender loyalty with all stakeholders.

A paradigm is like an operating system for a computer. The machine will only do what the operating system allows it to do. If your paradigms are from the past, you'll be using obsolete applications that aren't up to the requirements of today.

As the graphic below shows, you need an overarching "leadership operating system," like *The 7 Habits of Highly Effective People*, to run today's applications—the Paradigm Shifts we've listed. In this book, we're going to invite you to adopt a new leadership operating system and to "download" the Paradigm Shifts to your own mind.

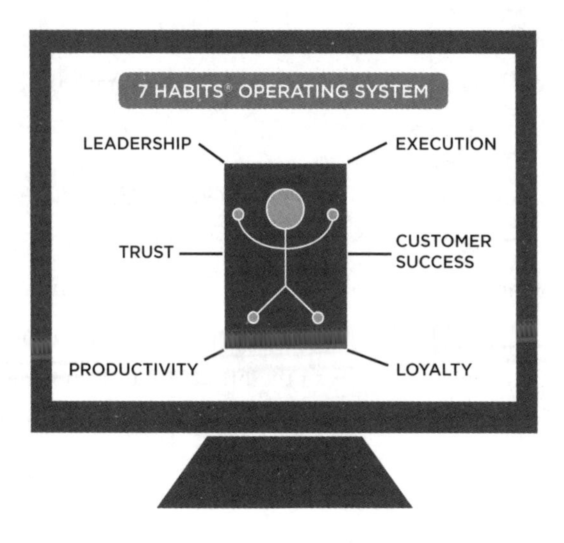

You will discover the key to a culture like the one that keeps the Bakerloo Line on track. By instilling *The 7 Habits of Highly Effective People* along with our other behavior-change solutions, we helped them build a culture of proactivity and resourcefulness. Around 100 million passengers ride the Bakerloo Line each year. The Bakerloo team succeeds in their increasingly demanding environment because of the kind of people they are, which is a reflection of the kind of leaders they have. The Bakerloo Line's highly effective leadership produced highly engaged people, and you can't calculate the value of that kind of engagement.

These Paradigm Shifts, practices, and operating system are absolutely fundamental to success *now*. Each requires changing people's hearts and minds in fundamental ways.

Changing behavior is about the hardest challenge anyone ever faces. (If you don't think so, just consider how hard it is for you to change *your* behavior.) It's a great challenge, but the shift must be made. This book will show you how. The paradigms of the past might have been good for the times, but you can't afford to live by them now. In the face of the public sector's growing competitive cauldron, you will lose the ultimate mission essential: people who bring talent, passion, determination, and focus to the success of your organization and its mission.

CHAPTER 3

THE NEED FOR LEADERS AT EVERY LEVEL

THE IMPORTANCE OF RELEASING THE POTENTIAL OF EVERY PERSON

-

"In the Industrial Age, leadership was a position. In the Knowledge Age, leadership is a choice."
–Stephen R. Covey

-

The most highly motivated people in any organization tend to be its leaders.

Leaders are the people who are responsible for results. They "own" the results, good or bad, so they're highly committed to producing the best results possible. Leaders are far more likely to take initiative and care about their goals than "followers" are. After all, followers are not responsible.

People who own things take care of them. They wash their cars, repair their homes, tend their gardens. They *take* care *because* they care. On the other hand, non-owners care little, if at all:

Who washes a rental car? No one.

Why? The person doesn't own it.

In government organizations, the leaders are owners; they own goals, projects, initiatives, and systems. A big challenge for leaders is to get other people—the non-owners—to care about those things. Many in government contend they are hindered in driving results because they cannot provide performance incentives or "fire" a poor performer like those in the private sector. There may be some truth to that argument; however, the reality is that followers—no matter the compensation; no matter the promises, benefits, or opportunities for advancement—simply don't care in the same way leaders do. Followers don't *own* anything.

A Brief History of Leadership and Management

Ever since the founding of the first government organization (whatever it was), leaders have struggled with this problem: How do you motivate people to give their best? Age after age of autocratic leaders used fear as the primary lever for engagement. Compliance was key. In the last century, scientific managers used the "carrot and stick" approach that was well suited to a population of workers with minimal education and low expectations. Then around mid-century, things changed. People became more educated and their expectations rose, forcing leaders to involve them more. That led to the rise of "participatory management," which was originally supposed to flatten out hierarchies and democratize the organization.

It didn't work. Just the opposite happened as bureaucracies grew, hierarchies became more entrenched, silos popped up everywhere, turf wars became the norm, and politics nosed into the relationships between leaders and followers.

We invite you to look around your organization and consider how (or if) that statement applies to your circumstance. What signs of entrenchment, silos, turf wars, and politics exist that are impeding progress on your mission?

You likely noted a few impediments—impediments that have negative consequences toward achieving your critical goals. No doubt your predecessors worked to overcome these challenges by creating organizational policies that grew larger and larger in an effort to address every issue that might arise. If leadership is defined as "someone who has a supervisory position," then the majority of your organization is likely comprised of "followers." And if almost everyone is a follower, you have to spell everything out for them. An overemphasis on Industrial Age-style hierarchies inevitably produced the psychological impact of knowing "I am not as important as you." No one moved until the "boss" told that person to do it. Matrix organizations were supposed to soften this impact, but they also generated confusion. The more complex the organization, the more helpless people felt. By the year 2000, in the words of some astute observers, there was a wave of "increasing urgency in the…frustration at all levels with pointless layers of hierarchy, egotistical leadership, autocratic decision making, and bureaucratic bungling."[11]

Now, many leaders—most importantly, government leaders—are frankly bewildered. They are caught between accomplishing a highly important mission and desperately trying to figure out how to lead and motivate followers: "Am I the boss or the best friend? Am I going to be a controlling manager or an empowering manager? Am I a 'Theory X' manager, handing down orders and showing who's boss, or am I a 'Theory Y' manager, nurturing, egalitarian, and sensitive? Am I the great visionary or the button-down analyst? Am I a systemizer or a humanist?"

Stanford Professor Harold Leavitt beautifully described today's leadership dilemma this way: "Humanizers focus on the people side of the organization, on human needs, attitudes, and emotions. They are generally opposed to hierarchies, viewing them as restrictive, spirit-draining, even imprisoning.

11. Kenneth Cloke and Joan Goldsmith, *The End of Management,* Jossey-Bass, 2002, 4.

Systemizers, in contrast, fixate on facts, measurements, and systems. They are generally in favor of hierarchies, treating them as effective structures for doing big jobs. Humanizers tend to stereotype systemizers as insensitive, anal-retentive types who think that if they can't measure it, it isn't there. Systemizers tend to caricature humanizers as fuzzy-headed, overemotional creatures who don't think straight."[12]

Of course, most managers vacillate back and forth across this spectrum as they develop a certain sense about which style to use, depending on the situation. Some try for a balance between distant boss and approachable colleague, but it's an extremely tough balance to strike. In practice, managers keep seesawing between the styles—somebody's floundering over there lacking necessary expertise, so you have to go micromanage them. Meanwhile, everybody else feels abandoned, other people start to flounder and, eventually, you're micromanaging *them*. And so it goes, as you run from one crisis to another.

Professor Leavitt concludes that this typical approach to organizational leadership "breeds infantilizing dependency, distrust, conflict, toadying, territoriality, distorted communication, and most of the other human ailments that plague every large organization."[13]

---

12. Harold Leavitt, *Top Down: Why Hierarchies Are Here to Stay and How to Manage Them More Effectively*, Harvard Business Press, 2005, 67.

13. Jeremy Pearce, "Harold J. Leavitt, 85, Management Expert, Dies," *The New York Times*, Dec. 26, 2007. http://www.nytimes.com/2007/12/26/business/26leavitt.html?_r=0

The problem, however, is not how to strike a balance between two dysfunctional styles of leading people: The problem is in your paradigm of a *leader.*

In government, leaders have always been defined by their titles. Military and law-enforcement personnel wear their ranks on their uniforms. Politicians and career civil servants are often referred to by their title or level instead of their actual name. It is not uncommon for someone to introduce himself or herself with a title consisting of several words, each creating more ambiguity around actual responsibilities. Stephen R. Covey often discussed how leaders aren't defined by their block on the organizational chart. The person on top is "no more likely to be a leader than anyone else." What he meant was that a grant of formal authority doesn't make you a leader. It makes you accountable, but owning a title doesn't make you a leader any more than owning a pair of skis makes you a downhill racer. A title doesn't automatically entitle you to anything.

A title doesn't automatically entitle you to anything.

Think about leadership in two ways: formal authority that comes with a title, and moral authority that comes with your character. As you look at the leaders you've known, you know some of them have had little influence despite their title. In fact, many on their teams are simply "waiting them out." The built-in churn among government leaders often fosters this mentality. On the other hand, there are the unofficial leaders everybody trusts.

The truth is that anyone can be a leader, regardless of title or job description. Gandhi energized the entire Indian nation and won its independence but never held a formal title. Every organization has an informal network of "go-to people" for wisdom, advice, and solutions. They are often neither senior leaders nor managers, but they have earned "informal authority" because of their experience and influence.

Having a few leaders deciding everything just bottlenecks the whole organization. Important issues often stack up waiting for a decision from the front office. Just think of how long it takes to get the boss to sign off on something. We have grown accustomed to this, assuming this is simply how government works. Gary Hamel challenges all organizations to rethink this mindset saying, "We still have these organizations where too much power and authority are reserved for people at the top of the pyramid.... We have to syndicate the work of leadership more broadly."[14]

---

14. "Leaders Everywhere: A Conversation With Gary Hamel," McKinsey Insights & Publications. May 2013. http://www.mckinsey.com/insights/organization/leaders_everywhere_a_conversation_with_gary_hamel

Everyone Leads

So if you want to motivate people, and leaders are the *most* motivated people, *why not make everyone a leader?*

It's entirely possible to create the conditions where everyone can be a leader if you change your paradigm of what a leader is. When you no longer think of leadership as the sole province of a few select people, you realize that all people have primary leadership qualities that can be leveraged. Initiative, resourcefulness, vision, strategic focus, creativity—these qualities are in no way limited to the front office. Even small children can become leaders.

Thousands of schools have adopted the 7 Habits as a way to teach leadership to children. Usually, "student leaders" are a small group of gifted, outgoing kids who are always the class officers, the top athletes, or the leads in the school play. But in schools we've worked with, *all* students are expected to be leaders. Every child is a leader of something. Organizing books, announcing the lunch menu, collecting homework, greeting guests, dispensing hand sanitizers—these might not seem like "leadership" roles, but leadership starts here. The children learn what it feels like to be responsible. They learn that being a leader means being a contributor.

Most students take huge pride in their responsibilities. Some don't want to miss a day because of their desire to fulfill their leadership roles. As they mature, so do their responsibilities: they take over marking attendance, teaching lessons, leading projects, mentoring other students, even grading homework. Every student can lead something. An autistic boy who struggles to keep track of time does small daily routines in the nurse's office. He is so excited to fill his leadership role that he watches the clock like a hawk and is never late for his job. Another boy with a history of discipline problems is assigned to lead the office staff in doing several tasks once a day. He not only shows up for his "shift," but comes back two or three times a day wanting to know if he can help; his discipline problems have evaporated.

These children will grow up seeing themselves as leaders no matter what "positions" they hold in their careers. They will understand the key difference between an office holder—or perhaps someone stuck with an additional duty—and a leader. They will learn to understand the difference between *formal* authority and *real* authority. This paradigm has had a profound impact on academic performance, which has dramatically increased over the time the school adopted this "leadership framework," and has led to a marked decrease in discipline issues. At the time of this writing, more than 3,500 schools have followed this model with remarkable results.

Patrick tells the story of an extraordinary government leader he had the opportunity to interact with over a twelve-year period. "In 1998, I was assigned to work on a project at a U.S. Air Force base. My work focused on studying and documenting highly complex financial-management processes. The project required me to meet with various subject-matter experts, conduct interviews to understand aspects of the overall process, connect the dots to define the entire system, and work with my teammates to create a handbook that would be used throughout the Department of Defense (DoD). In all honesty, the project was a bit daunting. After all, with a system that complex, where does one start?"

The first day on the job, Patrick met Rick and was informed that if he needed any guidance, Rick would point him in the right direction. "When we first met," Patrick explains, "I didn't realize that I was standing in the presence of the one of the best leaders and change agents I would ever meet. In hindsight, the initial introduction was rather prosaic. Rick was sitting in a cubicle space like everyone else in the building, had no 'block' on the organizational chart, and introduced himself using only his first name. He was friendly and said he was willing to help me if I needed anything."

As it turns out, in addition to being a wealth of knowledge about how Patrick could tackle his work, Rick was working on a major project of his own. Where Patrick's project was complex, Rick's assignment proved to be a tortuous labyrinth. He was tasked to define the Air Force's requirements for a multiservice computer system. The project required him to travel often, make recommendations to senior leaders, and keep his team on track as they worked to accomplish a number of high-visibility deliverables. Patrick later learned that while others ran from the thought of working on the project, Rick volunteered—he stepped up to lead his part of the endeavor. In doing so, he played an invaluable role in getting the solution right for the thousands who would use the system in the coming decades. While others were saying the project wouldn't work or would be too daunting, Rick took ownership.

If he had done this once, it would have been remarkable, but leading out on tough issues became a hallmark of Rick's careers. Over the next decade, Patrick saw Rick not just as one of a hundred program analysts working in a cubicle farm, but the one program analyst who chose to lead from where he sat and changed the trajectory of the organization. Rick volunteered his best and played active roles in creating a DoD-wide cost accounting system; establishing several workforce-development programs, including the certification of thousands of employees; and negotiating a relationship between the U.S. government and one of the nation's top universities to establish a graduate-studies program for high-potential government employees. Rick did not seek out formal leadership positions—in fact, he turned down the ones he was offered. Nonetheless, he was a strong leader, made huge contributions, owned numerous projects, mentored many people, led lots of teams, and left a legacy that is felt throughout the Air Force.

Rick knows the tremendous difference between a *leader* and a person who merely has formal authority. Anyone can be a leader who chooses to be, regardless of level or supervisory responsibilities, and the organization that knows how to help everyone make that choice will have an unbelievable advantage. An organization full of people like Rick is unstoppable!

You could argue that the main job of leaders is to create other leaders. But if everyone's a leader, you ask, who are the followers? That's easy. It's like asking, "At the schools we just discussed, is a particular child a teacher or a learner?" He is both. The same student teaches *and* learns, and in an organization, the same person leads *and* follows.

You could argue that the main job of leaders is to create other leaders.

What does it mean to have a culture where everyone is a leader?

It means that there's a common "leadership operating system"—a framework everyone in the organization shares. Your devices have an operating system, like Windows or the Apple OS. It makes everything else run. Without it, the device is just a dead piece of metal and plastic. Just as there's a common operating system on all your computers and standard operating procedures for your work, an organization has a *certain way of leading and of behaving.*

What is your leadership operating system? Does everyone in the organization know how to succeed? how to behave? how to problem-solve and innovate?

As we've seen, in most organizations, the current leadership operating system is flawed. Some are deeply flawed, where only big egos, tyrants, or passive-aggressives can thrive. But most leaders simply have an outdated paradigm: they're doing their best to take charge instead of inspiring others to take charge.

Most leaders simply have an outdated paradigm: they're doing their best to take charge instead of inspiring others to take charge.

The beginning structure of information technology is helpful here. In the old world, a big mainframe master computer dictated to subservient computers that simply did as they were told. That day is long gone. Now, we all have our own smartphones, laptops, and tablets, which are all connected to clouds brimming with information (much of which didn't even exist yesterday) that we can access with the swipe of a finger or a simple voice command.

Traditionally, to be "the leader" means to take the whole enterprise on your back; to be the boss, the head honcho, the big noise, the top brass—the "mainframe." It's an exhausting prospect. It's also terribly ineffective, to say the least. Here you are, surrounded by people with enormous talent, capability, experience, insight, and ingenuity, while you pretend to be the sole source of those things. We're still "leading" others as if we were back in an Industrial Age world. But now, we've reached a tipping point where that paradigm just won't work. It's time for a totally new leadership operating system that frees *everyone* to lead.

CHAPTER 4

THE OPERATING SYSTEM THAT BUILDS EFFECTIVE LEADERS AT EVERY LEVEL

ACCELERATING PERFORMANCE THROUGH THE POWER OF INTERDEPENDENCE

-

"We've gone through the operating system and looked at everything and asked how we can simplify this and make it more powerful at the same time."

–Steve Jobs

-

The 7 Habits in Our Operating System

What are the features of our new leadership operating system? What are the principles behind it? In 1989, Stephen R. Covey published *The 7 Habits of Highly Effective People*, which introduced a powerful yet implementable operating system for individual, team, and organizational leadership. Here are the attributes and behaviors of leaders who operate according to the 7 Habits:

1. **Proactivity.** They take initiative and responsibility for results (Habit 1).
2. **Purpose.** They Begin With the End in Mind® by having a sense of mission that is clear, compelling, and infectious (Habit 2).
3. **Priority.** They are highly productive, intensely focused on getting the right things done. They Put First Things First® (Habit 3).
4. **Mutual Benefit.** They "Think Win-Win®," showing deep respect and seeking always to benefit others as well as themselves (Habit 4).
5. **Empathy.** They are profoundly empathic, seeking to understand people and issues from many perspectives, guiding people with just-in-time coaching and feedback. Their influence increases as a result (Habit 5).
6. **Synergy.** They practice synergy, leveraging the capabilities and resources of people to create new solutions (Habit 6).
7. **Continuous Improvement.** They are always getting better and more capable, never satisfied to stand still. They Sharpen the Saw® (Habit 7).

Everyone should strive to have these leadership attributes. It doesn't matter what your title or job description may be, whether you are a seasoned senior executive or an freshly minted individual contributor. This operating system or framework allows everyone at any level in the organization to know what is expected and to succeed personally, interpersonally, and organizationally.

When Stephen R. Covey isolated these basic attributes as *The 7 Habits of Highly Effective People*, his book swept like wildfire around the world, with millions of copies on millions of bookshelves everywhere, from pole to pole and from Sao Paulo to Saudi Arabia. Today *The 7 Habits* book continues to jump off the shelves, with no formal marketing to support these sales. The book's message lingers in many people's minds today because it has never lost its timeless appeal, and many organizational leaders have accepted the challenge to create the conditions for turning *everyone* into a leader.

In July 2013, Jim Collins wrote the foreword to the 25th Anniversary Edition of *The 7 Habits* book. He wrote: "Stephen Covey was a master synthesizer. I think of what he did for personal effectiveness as analogous to what the graphical user interface did for personal computers. Prior to Apple and Microsoft, few people could harness computers to their daily lives; there was no easily accessible user interface—there were no mouse pointers, friendly icons, or overlapping windows on a screen, let alone a touch screen. But with the Macintosh and then Windows, the mass of people could finally tap the power of the microchip behind the screen. Similarly, there had been hundreds of years of accumulated wisdom about personal effectiveness, from Benjamin Franklin to Peter Drucker, but it was never assembled into one coherent, user-friendly framework. Covey created a standard operating system—the 'Windows'—for personal effectiveness, and he made it easy to use....

"The ideas embedded in the framework are timeless. They are *principles*. This is why they work and speak to people in all age groups around the globe. In a world of change, disruption, chaos, and relentless uncertainty, people crave an anchor point, a set of constructs to give them guidance in the face of turbulence."

Jim closes his forward by saying, "*The 7 Habits of Highly Effective People* is twenty-five years young, off to a very strong start indeed."

Let's look at the 7 Habits and what they bring to a leader's mindset, skillset, toolset.

The 7 Habits of Highly Effective People	**Basic Attributes of a Leader**
Be Proactive®	Take initiative and responsibility for results.
Begin With the End in Mind®	Have a clear vision and a sense of mission that is infectious.
Put First Things First®	Be highly productive, intensely focused on getting the right things done.
Think Win-Win®	Show deep respect, seeking always to benefit others as well as yourself.
Seek First to Understand, Then to Be Understood®	Be profoundly empathic, seeking to understand people and issues from many perspectives.
Synergize®	Practice synergy, seeing differences as sources of strength and leveraging the capabilities and resources of people to create new solutions.
Sharpen the Saw®	Continuously improve your capabilities.

One example of an organization that is successfully turning everyone into a leader is Mexico's MICARE mining company. The Mexican government started MICARE in

1977 and the mine began producing coal for energy in 1983. Seven days a week, twenty-four hours a day, 6,000 workers in MICARE's mines grind through coal seams 2,000 feet below the surface of the earth.

MICARE's only customer is the Mexican Federal Electricity Commission, which buys millions of tons of MICARE's coal to generate electricity at the nearby José Lopez Portillo electrical plant. From this effort, a full 10 percent of Mexico's electricity needs are met. A few years ago, however, production was beginning to drop even as demand for electricity was rising.

According to director Jorge Carranza Aguirre, "We were going through difficult times. We had to reduce costs while increasing production to meet higher demand. The problem was too much pressure, too much stress on people. Under these conditions, it was each man for himself. There was a lot of conflict between units and between workers and supervisors, and that created slowdowns. We did many good things, but we lacked unity and motivation.

"We had given the workers a lot of technical training and taught them how to operate the machines, but we needed to provide them with different kinds of tools. They needed to be able to manage themselves. When I heard about the 7 Habits, I realized this was the system I was looking for.

"The 7 Habits changed everybody's mindset. At the top, we realized that if we wanted to be a first-world company, we needed a new foundational principle—that people make the organization, and to the degree to which we strengthen the people, we will strengthen the organization. We wanted everyone to be a leader."

As we brought the managers and union leaders together around the 7 Habits, conflict decreased tremendously. Seeing themselves now as responsible leaders instead of victims, miners started taking initiative, setting goals, and collaborating on solutions to their own team and production issues.

Before long, the new culture was spilling over into the homes of the workers. People asked, in a good way, "What are they doing to my spouse at work! Now they're coming home, and they want to make Win-Win Agreements, they want to be more proactive, and they have a vision of what they want to do in life—things they never even thought of before." Eventually, entire families joined the *7 Habits* classes and the culture of the community was transformed. When asked what had changed about the MICARE miners, the wife of one miner replied, "Heart, heart, feeling…in every way, in the family and for their co-workers."

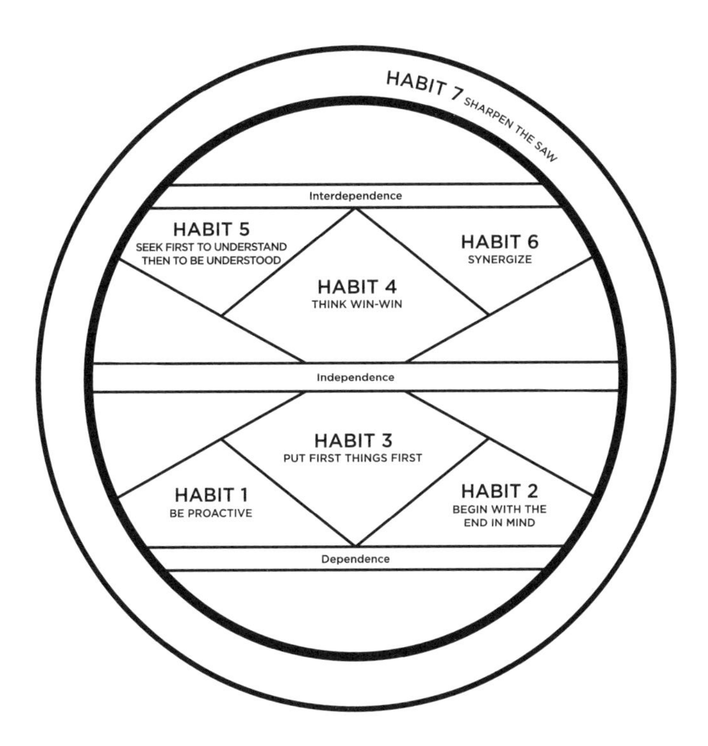

Today the 7 Habits are painted on the outside of virtually every building in the mining complex. Miners paste 7 Habits stickers onto their safety helmets before they descend into the mines. MICARE has captured minds *and* hearts as the 7 Habits become a standard "leadership operating system" for everyone.

How do you make the 7 Habits the personal operating system for everyone?

Given a Choice, Would People Choose to Follow You?

The job starts with you. It's time to evaluate your own leadership operating system. Jim Collins has said, "One of the most important variables in whether an enterprise remains great lies in a simple question: what is the *truth* about the inner motivations, character, and ambition of those who hold power?"[15] That's why this book is, first of all, about you. Whether you realize it or not, you hold power. You can be the pivot point between the past and the future for your group, team, or organization. It doesn't matter if you are the most senior leader or the newest entry-level person: regardless of your position, you can choose to lead out and help create the future, or you can let the opportunity pass.

The real question is what are *your* "inner motivations, character, and ambition"?

If you adopt the 7 Habits as your personal operating system, you can't help but become a leader. You'll behave the way a true leader behaves. The 7 Habits are a matter of character: they come from the inside out, which means you can't fake them on the surface. You can't pretend to be proactive or mission-driven or empathic with other people—they will spot your inconsistencies in a heartbeat. Practicing the 7 Habits means real introspection into your

15. Stephen Covey, *The 7 Habits of Highly Effective People,* (Simon & Schuster), 6.

own character and motives. This doesn't mean you need to be perfect at living the 7 Habits. People will forgive lapses as long as they know you're trying.

To really understand *The 7 Habits of Highly Effective People* and how to incorporate them into your life, you need to read the book. We're not going into depth on each habit here, but let's look at the 7 Habits as a personal operating system for leaders.

Habit 1—Be Proactive: Take Initiative and Responsibility for Results

The foundational habit of any true leader is to Be Proactive. It means you habitually take responsibility. You take initiative. You act instead of waiting to be acted upon. You're resourceful. You don't take no for an answer (at least not until there's absolutely no way to get a yes).

Proactivity is a simple yet profound principle, but many people have trouble with it. It's easier to be reactive and live on inertia than to stand up and lead out. We're uncomfortable with change and the people who want to change things. We discount our own abilities ("I'm not a natural leader; I don't know what to do; I don't have any influence around here").

The Wall Street Journal observes, "Most managers will spend their entire work life reacting to orders from above, reacting to pressures and problems from below, or simply reacting to the insistent demands of a busy workplace. If all you do is react, you will fail as a manager. You may be good at solving problems that arise. You may be skilled at responding to the needs and requests of those you work for or the people on your team. You may work long hours, be loved and respected by your employees and be the very model of organizational efficiency. But you will not be an effective manager."[16]

Effective leaders are proactive, not reactive. They are passion-driven and resourceful and they find a way to achieve what matters most.

In the film *Dead Poets Society,* a group of boys start classes at a private school in New England. On the first day, the wide-eyed and anxious boys proceed in a very orderly way from chemistry class to Latin to trigonometry, listening quietly to the standard initiation speeches from each teacher. Finally, they meet their new English teacher, Mr. Keating. He asks a boy to open the literature textbook and read aloud the introduction, a dry essay on the science of interpreting poetry. As the boy reads, it becomes clear that Mr. Keating

16. "How to Set Goals for Employees," *The Wall Street Journal*, n.d. http://guides.wsj.com/management/strategy/how-to-set-goals/

does not like what he is hearing. He stops the boy and asks him to rip the introduction out of the book.

The boys stare at him in amazement. He then orders them all to rip those pages from their books as if the very presence of the essay alongside the works of Keats and Blake and Wordsworth and Shakespeare threatens their power and meaning. The teacher gathers the boys close to him and in hushed, dramatic tones declares, "We don't read poetry because it is cute. We read it because we are members of the human race, and the human race is filled with passion!"

It's the essence of leadership to be passionate. There is a science of leadership, but it's secondary to the hunger and thirst to make a difference, to make a contribution that matters. If you are not passionately engaged in your work, you might ask yourself why. If others are not passionately engaged, it's essential to find out why.

Great leaders have the "passion to see it through," as Seth Godin says. "The willingness to find a different route when the first one doesn't work. The certainty that in fact, there is a way, and you care enough to find it. This is a choice, not something you get certified in."[17] While proactive people are passionate, they are also resourceful. Proactivity means you *find a way*.

---

17. Seth Godin, "Choosing to Be Formidable," *Seth's Blog*, Aug. 9, 2013. http://sethgodin.typepad.com/seths_blog/2013/08/choosing-to-be-formidable.html

More than a century ago, a young African-American woman named Mary McLeod Bethune started the "Daytona Literary and Industrial Training School for Negro Girls" in Daytona, Florida. The fifteenth child of former slaves, Mary grew up in deep poverty, but with her passion for learning, she pleaded for a place in school and eventually became a teacher. Recognizing that black girls of that time and place had little opportunity for an education, she became fired up with the idea of starting her own school for them.

Mary's cash resources consisted of $1.50, but that didn't stop her. Her resources were limited only by her ingenuity, and that was unlimited. The only place she could find for her school was a shack next to the town dump, so she cleaned it up and used it. There was no money for supplies, so she made desks out of old boxes, pencils from charred wood, and ink out of boiled-down berry juice. Her desk was a packing case. "I lay awake at nights, contriving how to make peach baskets into chairs."[18]

The school opened in 1904 with five eager girls, six books, and the devoted Mary McLeod Bethune as the teacher. While teaching reading, writing, and math, she also taught them to be as resourceful as she was. What could they do to help support the school? One girl knew how to make a mattress by stuffing it with moss. Others knew how to bake

18. Bernice Anderson Poole, *Mary McLeod Bethune*, Holloway House Publishing, 1994, 145.

pies. So they made and sold mattresses to their neighbors and offered pieces of sweet potato pie to the tourists who descended on Daytona Beach for the auto races. That's how they paid the $11 monthly rent on their school. "I considered cash money as the smallest part of my resources," Mary later wrote. "I had faith in a loving God, faith in myself, and a desire to serve."[19] Mary's little school eventually grew into Bethune-Cookman University, thriving today with nearly 4,000 students and a $34 million endowment.

No one who knows the story of Mary McLeod Bethune can talk with a straight face about being short on resources. Our own ingenuity is the greatest of our resources, but only proactive people can leverage that resource. How resourceful are you? How resourceful are the people around you? Or do you live in a culture of helplessness, constantly restrained by a lack of passion and resources from making the great contribution you are capable of?

Habit 2—Begin With the End in Mind: Gain a Clear Sense of Mission

The second foundational habit of any true leader is to have a clear "end in mind," a vision or mission that inspires and energizes you. It also means that you have a clear

19. Glenn J. Browne and Ray B. Browne, "Mary McLeod Bethune," in *Contemporary Heroes and Heroines*, Book II, ed. Deborah Straub. (Gale Research, 1992; Poole), 151–152.

purpose in mind for everything you do—initiatives, projects, meetings. It's based on the simple principle of knowing your destination early. Even if you fall short, you'll be moving in the right direction.

Some people say, "All the talk about vision is just drivel." However, everything made by humans is the result of a vision, from a potato peeler to the *Mona Lisa*. It's designed in the mind first. Ironically, we know how to design potato peelers, but we're not very good at designing a life. By just taking things as they come, we go at the most important things in life without much vision.

How often do we hear (and sometimes say), "They don't know what they're doing in the head office. This organization is drifting. Does anybody know where we're headed?" Employees sit in meetings and nod their heads as the senior leader discusses his or her plans. They attend town halls and listen to someone wax on about the next iteration of the organization's mission statement, thinking that it sounds eerily similar to the last one. They watch organizational lines being drawn and redrawn, only to encounter the same problems a year later. They listen to organizational plans that seem void of passion, vision, or even sense. Throughout all of this, people lose sight of what they are truly trying to achieve.

It sounds so obvious: "What is it that we are trying accomplish? Does it make sense? Is there any passion at all, any aspiration in it? How will we measure success?" But it's remarkable how many managers never even ask these basic questions. And if they do think about them, they're afraid to ask because, after all, they should know, shouldn't they?

Even fewer ask themselves, "What is my own personal mission? What should I contribute here? What kind of a difference do I want to make? What will I remember about my work here? How will people remember me—or will they remember me at all?" Or do they see themselves as "job descriptions with legs," giving little or nothing of their own mind and heart to their work?

"The human race is filled with passion," Mr. Keating said to the boys in *Dead Poets Society*. He then quotes the great Walt Whitman, answering that his purpose in life is "That the powerful play goes on and you may contribute a verse." Mr. Keating then asks, "What will your verse be?"

What a wonderful and appropriate question for each of us to consider. What will our individual "verses" be? How will we make our contributions to the world?

Creating—or better said, *discovering*—your personal mission is a difficult but very powerful process. It will help bring clarity to the things you value and will help define how you spend your time and the contributions you will make. It will bring a greater sense of meaning to your work. You'll be able to help your team craft its mission. You might even influence your organization's mission.

When Mary McLeod Bethune was campaigning for her school one day, she bravely introduced herself at a palatial vacation house in Daytona Beach and was received by the old gentleman who owned it. He enjoyed her gift of sweet potato pie and kept asking her back, which delighted her. She talked about her school in radiant terms, about the library and the chapel and the schoolrooms and the lovely, uniformed girls. "I would like you to become one of the school's trustees," she told him.

One day, his big limousine arrived unannounced at the school. The old gentleman got out, looked around, and saw nothing but a shed in a muddy field. One girl read aloud from a geography book while others peeled and boiled sweet potatoes for pie. Mary took off her apron and looked the man straight in the eye.

"And where is this school that you wanted me to be a trustee of?" he asked. He was obviously not pleased.

Mary smiled up at him and said, "In my mind and in my soul."

After a moment's hesitation, James Norris Gamble, a founder of Procter & Gamble and the fabulously wealthy inventor of Ivory soap, wrote her a check. Overwhelmed by the power of her vision, Gamble provided a means for realizing that vision for the rest of his life.

But the school was only a part of her vision. "The drums of Africa still beat in my heart," she said. "They will not let me rest while there is a single Negro boy or girl without a chance to prove his worth."[20] With Gamble's support and that of many others, Mary McLeod Bethune served as a remarkable agent of change for African-American people. She helped found the National Association of Colored Women to help Black people register to vote (which earned her a few visits from the Ku Klux Klan). She became the first female head of a U.S. federal agency, the "Division of Negro Affairs," as a close advisor to President Franklin D. Roosevelt and his wife Eleanor. Finally, she was the only Black woman present at the founding of the United Nations.

Again, Habit 2 starts with you. What is your mission or vision of your own future? What will your contribution be in your current work role? Once you have discovered and carefully defined your personal mission, you have a clear "end in mind" and you can begin to influence others to make their contributions, as Mary McLeod Bethune did.

---

20. Poole, 130, 152–153.

Habit 3—Put First Things First: Focus on Getting the Right Things Done

The third foundational habit of any true leader is to prioritize so you're also giving the most attention to what's most important. This is easy to do if you already know what the mission is. Without the mission, you literally can't tell what the first things are.

And that's the problem with many leaders. Yes, they may know the organization's mission statement, but they're unclear on the end state or destination; they can't distinguish between what is "wildly important" and what is merely an "urgent priority." Many so-called urgent priorities are neither urgent nor priorities: they are momentary distractions that actually prevent leaders from achieving the mission.

On a hot September day in 2005, wildfire erupted in Topanga Canyon, California. Only a mountain ridge separated the huge fire from Los Angeles and a major disaster seemed likely. One of the United States' largest cities could have been consumed, but it didn't happen. The damage was limited because the Los Angeles County Fire Department had long since "Put First Things First."

Most people would say that the mission of a fire department is to put out fires. The L.A. County Fire Department didn't see it that way: their mission was to prevent damage to life and property. They didn't want to fight any fires; they never wanted to deal with a fire at all. So they had adopted aggressive goals long before, goals to educate the public about making "defensible space" around their homes, clearing brush, removing fire hazards, and creating safe zones. They had pursued this goal intently and, as a result, the Topanga Canyon Fire was far less destructive than it might have been. The Los Angeles County Fire Department never has to fight a fire they've already prevented.

By contrast, most leaders spend most of their time "fighting fires." You hear it all the time—people are "insanely busy" trying to keep up with urgent demands on their time and never catching up, never getting on top of it all.

So, what is more important than fighting a fire? *Preventing the fire in the first place.*

That's the "first thing" that needs to be put first. If the mission is to preserve life and property, the goal must be not to fight fires but to keep them from breaking out.

As *The Wall Street Journal* says, "'What should we do?' is the first question the manager must answer. 'What is the mission of the organization I am managing? What is the strategy for accomplishing that mission? What are my goals for the future, consistent with strategy and mission? What are the overall goals for my team and for each member of the team?' "[21] Once the mission is clear (Habit 2), the leader's job is to set clear goals for achieving the mission (Habit 3).

Remember the principle of "no involvement, no commitment."

When a leader merely dictates the team's purpose without involving others in the process, that leader will find a low level of commitment and a high level of burnout from others. At the same time, you can't just rely on the input of others as the sole basis of your direction. A leader is more than a census taker. In fact, it's impossible to please all the people all the time, so don't even try. Involve people in key decisions, let them help you clarify the direction of the team or the initiative, but be prepared to take a stand once you have gathered data and input. Your shared mission is your guide to determining what truly are the "first things."

So, what are your "first things"? What goals must you set to achieve your mission? Just as important, what goals can you say no to?

---

21. "How to Set Goals," The *Wall Street Journal*, n.d. http://guides.wsj.com/management/strategy/how-to-set-goals/

Habit 4—Think Win-Win: Provide Mutual Benefit by Respectfully Seeking to Benefit Others as Well as Yourself

The fourth foundational habit of any true leader is to Think Win-Win. The basic principle here is respect for others *and* for yourself. No enduring arrangement in your work—or in life, actually—can succeed unless all parties are winning, especially in the long term.

"But sometimes our very job is to deny other people a win. We regulate, enforce, and say no," you say. "Whenever we tell someone or some organizations they can't do what they want, then we are winning and they are losing." And you're right, in independent situations when a regulation is enforced, one side may feel like it lost. But even in situations that seem highly combative, the enforcement of a building code might frustrate a construction company today but make them grateful down the road when a hurricane hits and their building survives the storm. Sure, the builder may never come to city hall to thank the inspectors, but virtually everything you do and every relationship you have depends on helping someone else succeed.

The basic leadership principle is that you don't succeed unless others succeed as well; therefore, win-win is the only rational way for a leader to think. Do you consider yourself a "win-win thinker"? What evidence do you have?

Would other people say that about you? Do you work in a win-win culture?

Habit 5—Seek First to Understand, Then to Be Understood: Empathize in Order to Understand People and Their Perspectives

The fifth foundational habit of any true leader is to seek first to understand other people before you try to make yourself understood. The basic principle here is *empathy*—putting yourself in the place of others so you can know and feel what they know and feel.

Why is empathy a crucial habit for a leader?

Picture a museum curator with no empathy for her patrons—how long will she keep the doors open if she remains totally disconnected from their needs? How about a project leader with no empathy for his team members? Or a teacher with no empathy for his students? An aeronautical engineer with no empathy for the crew on the plane she's designing? A hospital administrator with no empathy for the patients?

Obviously, most leaders have some empathy already. The problem is not that they can't understand people, but that they feel they must solve all their problems. Most leaders have a compulsion to fix everything at best and smooth things over at worst. It's a natural urge to want to jump in and save the day—to be the answer to everyone's problems. As one government executive told us, "Everyone knows how to bow down to the leader and tell them what they think the leader wants to hear." The problem is that many public-sector leaders spend too much time telling and not enough time listening. Of course, it's important to get to a solution, but you can't solve a problem you don't understand.

"I don't have time to listen," says the notorious alpha leader. "I already know what the problem is and I know how to solve it. My brain is way ahead of theirs. Time is precious. Why should I waste it sitting and listening to people?"

You practice Habit 5 just by listening—nothing else. You listen without interrupting, judging, analyzing, or answering back in your head. You're not thinking about what you're going to say next. Instead, you're listening closely both to what the person is saying and to what he or she is feeling.

Your goal is to understand. If you're a leader, *that's your job*. You can't connect with stakeholders and colleagues without empathy and understanding. Only by getting into the shoes of others can you serve them in a customized way—the way *they* want to be served.

Only an empathic leader can unleash the potential of other people. Leaders without empathy are literally working in the dark because they're ignorant of the passions, talents, and skills of their team members. You can't possibly discover and capitalize on the motivations of another human being without knowing the person deeply. For instance, as Professor Heidi Halvorsen says, some people eagerly embrace big, grand goals, while others are wary and skeptical, preferring more vigilance and less risk. Unless you know the "motivational fit" of each team member, you'll make poor choices about motivating them; the only way to uncover that motivational fit is to listen and understand.[22]

Empathy is essential to effective leadership, and it can't be faked. Stephen R. Covey said, "Leaders who take an interest in people merely because they should will be both wrong and unsuccessful. They will be wrong because regard for people is an end in itself. They will be unsuccessful because they will be found out."

For many, empathy is counterintuitive. In fact, among the hundreds of thousands of people we have assessed on various leadership and effectiveness principles, this is the least practiced and, not surprisingly, most requested skill.

---

22. See Heidi Halvorsen and E. Tory Higgins, *Focus: Use Different Ways of Seeing the World for Success and Influence*, Hudson Street Press, 2013.

Habit 6—Synergize: Leverage the Gifts and Resources of Other People

The sixth foundational habit of any true leader is to Synergize with other people. The basic principle here is *the whole is greater than the sum of its parts.* A team of people with diverse skills and perspectives is always more productive and creative than each member alone can be, not to mention the lone leader trying to figure things out in isolation. One plus one equals three, or ten, or a thousand. Consider, how many pounds can one draft horse pull? Answer: about 1,000 pounds. How many pounds can two draft horses pull? Answer: about 4,000 pounds. In this case, 1 + 1 = 4. That's simple math that is not always so simple. Why this result? The two horses, pulling together, compensate for the other's weaknesses. They complement each other; they fill in performance gaps. Each horse on its own is powerful. Together, their strength is remarkable!

When titles are conferred on people, they tend to become overcontrolling without realizing it. Their identity gets tied up in the phrase "I'm in charge here." They value sameness, so they squelch ideas from the members of their team. They want order, so they enforce uniformity of opinion. They want their way, so they discount the divergent views of the team, and synergy is suppressed.

We know one leader who was infatuated with his spot on the organizational chart. There were only a few blocks above his and numerous blocks below. He would spend the majority of his day running from meeting to meeting and his direct reports would wait for his return. In the past, when his team members demonstrated proactivity and stepped out on their own, he would attack their efforts and tell them he would have done it differently or not have done it at all. As a result, no one moved unless he told them to do so. His people learned not to take initiative. They had become risk-adverse, despite their apparent capabilities, ingenuity, or potential. Teamwork was nonexistent. The boss had fostered a group of mindless employees who waited for instructions—and hated their work.

The great irony here is that synergy is the reason for having a team in the first place. No individual is like any other; each has gifts, talents, passion, and skills no one else can duplicate. Effective leaders leverage those differences.

Consider what happens when Airbus Industrie puts together a team of biologists, physiologists, artists, molecular physicists, graphic designers, psychologists (and an aeronautical engineer or two) in a room and asks them to come up with the airplane of the future. What they envision will completely revolutionize air travel.

Imagine an airplane that mimics a human skeleton—it can twist, turn, spring, and vault like an athlete. Instead of wearing out, the plane's muscular shell actually gets stronger with stress, just like human muscles do. Its parts look like human bones. The mechanism of a baggage compartment is modeled on your shoulder joints. When you sit down, your seat molds itself around your body to give you a customized ride. Instead of a dim, dense atmosphere, the cabin is spacious and bathed in natural light: The skin of the airplane transmits light and energy and even data, carrying music and video and virtual golf games to the passengers. And the entire plane is organically grown from nanotubes—an enormous 3D printout weighing half of what our most advanced airplanes weigh.

"The airplane of the future will get its own consciousness," the designers say. "It will be more like a living organism than just a collection of very complex technology."[23]

This is the power of a synergistic team, where each individual member's skills, genius, and energy are leveraged to produce a marvel no one could have produced alone. On this team, every member is a leader.

"Wait," you say. "How can everybody on a team be a leader?"

---

23. Bastian Schaefer, "A 3D-Printed Jumbo Jet?" *TEDGlobal*, July 2013. http://www.ted.com/talks/bastian_schaefer_a_3d_printed_jumbo_jet.html

Imagine a team where everyone *is* a leader, where every member is proactive and visionary with clearly shared priorities. Imagine a team where everyone is looking out for the interests of each other, where they are intensely empathic and open to different views—in short, a team where the 7 Habits are the operating system. That is the team you need *now*.

Do you tend to welcome different points of view, or do you discourage them? Are you territorial, defensive, or closed to the ideas of others? Are you suffering from the "not invented here" syndrome? Or is your team a model of synergy? Do team members feel unleashed or chained back?

Habit 7—Sharpen the Saw: Keep Getting Better and More Capable; Never Stand Still

The seventh foundational habit of a true leader is to continuously improve your capabilities instead of letting them wear out. It's based on the principle that if you neglect yourself—your physical health, your learning, or your relationships—you will become dull and useless like an overused saw. Of course, any organization that doesn't continuously improve its capabilities will inevitably fade away, but continuous improvement starts with you. The whole mindset behind the "Sharpen the Saw" habit is that continual learning and growth are as essential to the individual as they are to the organization.

In many public-sector organizations, employees have become so entrenched with how they have historically done things that they fail to look for better ways to perform. Sure, some have tried to implement continuous improvement efforts like Total Quality Management or Six Sigma. Although laudable, few of these efforts have managed to become ingrained in the culture. This often occurs not because the initiative was a bad idea, but because the implementation approach was flawed. You can't set up an office to manage these initiatives and expect the culture to be driven by an isolated team separate from the leaders and team members who touch the work every day. This outside-in approach simply doesn't work. Putting it simply, you can't outsource sharpening the saw. After all, what happens when the continuous improvement effort stalls or runs headlong into another goal?

Maybe you are saying, "That might be true for other organizations, but we are flexible, nimble, alert to change, and constantly improving everything we do."

If that's true, then you are the exception. A global survey of companies in all major industries finds that more than 60 percent have tried and failed to implement continuous improvement systems, and that doesn't even count those who haven't tried. Those who have succeeded cite leadership commitment by far as the major reason for their success, and those who have failed (surprise!) overwhelmingly point to leaders' lack of commitment as the cause of the failure (88 percent!).[24]

Do you work for a "Sharpen the Saw" organization? Does your own team have a systematic approach to improving what you do? Do you have evidence that your core processes are getting better all the time?

And what about yourself—are you mentally and physically sharp? Are you a "continuous learner"? Do you work to keep your most important relationships healthy?

Putting It All Together: Installing the 7 Habits as Your Personal Operating System

An operating system is a set of rules that govern behavior. With a strong operating system like Windows or iOS or Android working in the background, you can smoothly run many applications, stay connected to the world, and feel secure.

A leadership operating system should do the same. It's the set of rules that govern your behavior as a leader. You

---

24. J.V. Kovach, et al. "The Use of Continuous Improvement Techniques: A Survey-Based Study of Current Practices," *International Journal of Engineering, Science and Technology*, vol. 3, no. 7 (2011), 89–100.

should be able to apply it confidently to any challenge or problem. It must allow you to connect to the world and stay relevant. You should have confidence that it works and will not fail you.

All of these standards are met by the 7 Habits. "How do you build leaders?" asks Jim Collins. "You first build character. And that is why I see the 7 Habits not just about personal effectiveness, but about leadership development."[25] With the 7 Habits as your leadership operating system, you'll be prepared to deal with today's chaotic, unpredictable world and anything it can throw at you. Your connections to the important people in your work and personal life will flourish. And the security of the system is unquestionable because it is founded in principles that are universal and never change.

How do you install the 7 Habits as your personal operating system? Pretty much the same way you'd install an operating system on your computer: by downloading it. Read Covey's classic book. Take the course. Find out how it feels to be more proactive, to have a clear vision for your own life, to unload a bagful of useless "priorities." Discover what happens when you approach people with a win-win mindset, when you stop trying to "fix" them and just understand them, and when you welcome their unique contribution to your life and work.

---

25. *The 7 Habits*, 4.

If you practice the 7 Habits, you won't need a fancy title to be a leader—you'll become a leader naturally.

Now, how do you help turn other people into leaders? As Gary Hamel asks, "What can we do to help teach people what it means to exercise leadership when they don't have formal authority?"[26] In other words, how do you install the 7 Habits operating system *into other people?*

Whole teams and organizations have been transformed by getting educated together on the 7 Habits. Some leaders have actively implemented the 7 Habits as a standard of behavior. Your influence might not extend that far right now. But as you model the 7 Habits in your own work, as the principles bear abundant fruit in your life, people will notice and your influence will inevitably grow. You'll find them following your example—which makes you a leader.

But you can do much more than model the 7 Habits. At the end of this chapter are instructions for doing a mental "download" of the 7 Habits operating system with your team. Follow the instructions carefully, and you'll be doing the job you need to do *now*. We have been influenced by many global leaders who have installed the 7 Habits operating system with great deliberation and thoughtfulness. They have taught us the importance of a leader's commitment to living the 7 Habits, to modeling them consistently, to

26. Hamel, "Leaders Everywhere."

installing systems in alignment with the principles, and to coaching performance consistently.

Listen to John Kotter, legendary Harvard professor of strategy: "The central issue [of leadership] is never strategy, structure, culture, or systems. The core of the matter is always about changing the behavior of people."[27] The way to change their behavior is to change their paradigms—to adopt an effective leadership operating system—and no priority is more important for you right now.

The 7 Habits Operating System: Instructions for Downloading

Here are seven commitments you can make right now—today—as you start your personal journey of becoming a more effective leader who models to others how they can become highly effective leaders as well:

27. Kotter, J. P., & Cohen, D. S. (2002). *The Heart of Change*. Boston: Harvard Business School Publishing.

<table>
<tr><th>Principle</th><th>Commitment</th></tr>
<tr><td rowspan="2">Proactivity</td><td>Get into the habit of taking initiative. Use proactive language.
Stop saying:

“I can’t do that, we don’t have the resources.”

“They won’t let us.”

“I’m not responsible.”

Say instead:

“I can do that.”

“I can find the resources.”

“We haven’t talked to the right people yet.”

“I’m responsible for my life and my work—no one else.”</td></tr>
<tr><td>What is a situation where I can be more proactive today?</td></tr>
</table>

Principle	Commitment
Vision	**Get into the habit of knowing the purpose for everything.** Begin everything with this thought: "What's the end in mind here? Why am I/ are we doing this?" Do this before you start projects, meetings, conferences, messages, documents—anything you do at work.
	What is a situation where I need to define my end in mind today?
	Design your future. How do you see yourself in a year? five years? ten years? How do you see your team or organization? What is your real mission? What do you want people to say about you when you're gone? Write these things down.
	How do I see my personal mission as of today?

Principle	Commitment
Productivity	**Get into the habit of doing only the things that are truly important and dropping those that aren't.** Plan your work weeks so your calendar fills with top priorities instead of secondary priorities. Ask yourself how you will carry out your vision or mission this week.
	What can I stop doing today?

Principle	Commitment
Mutual Benefit	**Get into the habit of thinking about how to benefit other people as well as yourself.** Who can help you carry out your vision or mission? What's in it for them? Make Win-Win Agreements with those people in which you spell out the wins for everyone.
	Where am I winning at someone else's expense? **Where is someone else winning at my expense?**

Principle	Commitment
Empathy	**Get into the habit of really listening.** Stop talking. Listen with empathy, which means dropping your own agenda and fully getting into theirs. (This doesn't mean you have to agree with their agenda; just understand it.) Do this with your co-workers, supervisors, and customers. Seek to understand them before giving your views.
	Who needs me to listen to them today?

Principle	Commitment
Synergy	**Get into the habit of looking for the solution you haven't thought of before.** Stop defending your territory and your "solutions." In problem solving, say to others, "What if we looked for a solution we haven't thought of before—a solution that's better than anything we've come up with yet? What would it look like?"
	What situation needs a synergistic solution today?

Principle	Commitment
Continuous Improvement	**Get into the habit of getting better—physically, mentally, spiritually, and in your relationships.** What can you do to keep up your energy and keep your mind sharp? What do you need to learn to do your job better? What relationships do you need to work on? If you are a "dull saw" instead of a "sharp saw," you won't really be a leader at all.
	Where do I need to "Sharpen the Saw" today?

You can do more formal things to download this mental operating system, including reading the book *The 7 Habits of Highly Effective People*. You can also get assessments and training to implement the habits more deeply into your team or organization.

CHAPTER 5

PRACTICE 1: LEAD WITH PURPOSE

A COMPELLING MISSION IS THE CATALYST FOR ENGAGEMENT

-

"Effort and courage are not enough without purpose and direction."
–John F. Kennedy

-

In Mumbai, India, a city of 22 million people, fast food has a unique meaning.

Every day, about 5,000 dabbawalas, or "lunchbox people," deliver nearly a quarter of a million home-cooked lunches around this vast, tumultuous city—at high speed *and without error!*

Because people who work in the city enjoy a home-cooked lunch, thousands of white-capped dabbawalas pick up the lunches in characteristic stacked lunchboxes, called "dabbas," from nearly a quarter of a million homes in the suburbs between 9 and 10 a.m. The mission: to get this specific lunch by lunchtime to a specific person downtown who is hungry for a hot meal. And it arrives every day—exactly at 12:30 p.m.

"The mission of the dabbawalas is not couched in flowery words...their simple goal is to serve their customers accurately and on time, every time."[28] They also have a unique value proposition: Unlike fast food chains, they bring a fresh, home-cooked lunch right to *you,* no matter where you are.

People with a simple, unique, powerful mission are the most engaged people. "To the moon," said John F. Kennedy. "Insanely great," said Steve Jobs. "There is a place in God's sun for the youth farthest down," said Mary Bethune, and her mission was to help them reach that place.

People with a simple, unique, powerful mission are the most engaged people.

Yet, the whole notion of "mission" has produced a lot of cynicism. There are two reasons for that: (1) too many mission statements are meaningless platitudes, and (2) people in the organization don't live up to the mission.

28. Sarah Sturtevant, "Lessons From a Dabbawala," *Marketing Masala,* June 10, 2009. http://sarahsturtevant.com/wordpress/branding/lessons-from-a-dabbawala/

Find the Voice of the Organization

There's a huge paradox here. A mission statement is supposed to express the passion of the people who are on the mission; yet, contests are held online for the "worst mission statement." People roll their eyes when anyone refers to the organization's mission statement. The bronze "mission statement" plaque becomes a target for pigeons. According to Gallup, *71 percent of U.S. government workers are disengaged—unimpressed and uninterested in their organization's mission.*[29]

Why are many mission statements just backroom jokes? Because of the tremendous irony in trying to engage people's passions and talents in a mission they have no passion for and no involvement in.

At the same time, there is nothing more powerful than the passions that drive people. Tap into those, and you create an unstoppable force. If you get people talking about their passions, they go so far overboard you can't get them to stop. But then management boils out all the passion to reduce it to a mediocre, bureaucratic-sounding mission statement, and that's why the cynicism.

---

29. *State of the American Workplace: Employee Engagement Insights for U.S. Business Leaders*, The Gallup Organization, 2013. http://www.gallup.com/strategicconsulting/163007/state-american-workplace.aspx

Without an engaging mission, the organization has no reason to exist. People in the organization struggle with an existential problem: they don't know what it all means, so they don't much care. There is nothing for them to engage with.

Without an engaging mission, the organization has no reason to exist.

Shawn: I was working with a group of leaders from an organization once where I noticed that on the wall of their conference room was beautifully framed copy of their mission statement. I read it. The words were nice and the sentiment meaningful. With this group of leaders all sitting around the large boardroom table and the framed mission statement just a few feet away, I said, "On the wall is your beautifully framed mission statement. Don't look at it. Who can tell me what it says?" Crickets. "Who can tell me the gist of what it says?" Again, crickets. What followed was an interesting discussion on what a mission statement really is and how individuals and organizations bring it to life.

Seth Godin says, "It's so easy to string together a bunch of platitudes and call them a mission statement. But what happens if you actually have a specific mission?"

Your true mission is discovered, not created, and it takes considerable effort to discover it. It is not a weekend's work. There's a universal quality in a great mission statement. You sense that it really matters to people, while at the same time there's nothing more distinctive, unique, or peculiar. It's generally applicable and unbelievably specific at the same time.

Your true mission is discovered, not created.

In broad strokes, it sounds something like this:

> We are going where no other people can go because no other people are like us. No one else has the unique combination of talent, passion, and conscience that drives us. No one else can make the contribution we can make.

The dabbawalas are like that. They are intensely proud of the service they have given for more than a century, a service no one can duplicate. Other great companies are like that. Passion for the mission governs everything they do: According to Mark Zuckerberg, "Facebook was not originally created to be a company. It was built to accomplish a social mission—to make the world more open and connected." So the company draws people with energy for that mission.

A great mission is expressed in negatives: "No one else goes there…no one else *can* go there…no one else is like us…no one else can contribute this…" There is absolutely no whisper of "me too." As Warren Buffett says, "The difference between successful people and really successful people is that really successful people say no to almost everything." When you say no to certain things, it allows you to say yes to other things—to the things that are in alignment with your mission.

"[R]eally successful people say no to almost everything."
—Warren Buffett

So call it what you want. If people are allergic to the term "mission statement," call it a mantra or a manifesto or a purpose statement or a passion statement or "the voice of the organization." Whatever you call it, you need it badly. The old paradigm of management is to put a mission statement on the wall and forget about it; the new paradigm of leadership is to help people find their voice—both individually and collectively. If you are not currently in position to "take on the mission statement of your organization," we strongly recommend that you master identifying the job to be done by your team.

The job used to be...	The job you must do now...
Put up a mission statement on the wall.	Find the voice of the organization.

Designing an Engaging Mission

How do you design a mission or a sense of purpose that will *engage* everyone?

The mission should be the collective voice of the people in your organization, not just the leader's voice. Of course, as leader, you are not just an opinion pollster—you do your own rigorous thinking and analysis about the mission. But you are not a dictator either. Everyone should be involved in creating it. The principle of "no involvement, no commitment" clearly applies to the creation of a mission statement. Leaders might "go off to the mountain" to create a vision, but that vision only becomes an organizational mission when people sign up to make it real. If you want everyone to own the mission, to lead out with it, they've got to have a say in it. It has to reflect their thinking, it has to express their potential, and it has to appeal to their soul.

Stephen R. Covey described the pathway to the promising side of today's reality as "the voice of the human spirit—full of hope and intelligence, resilient by nature, boundless in its potential to serve the common good...encompasses the soul of organizations that will survive, thrive, and profoundly impact the future of the world."[30]

How do you find this "voice of the organization"?

Dr. Covey explained, "Voice lies at the nexus of *talent* [what we do well], *passion* [what we love to do], *conscience* [what we ought to do], and *need* [what the world will pay us to do]."[31]

"Voice lies at the nexus of talent...passion...conscience...and need." —Stephen R. Covey

30. Stephen R. Covey, *The 8th Habit: From Effectiveness to Greatness,* Simon & Schuster, 2004, 5.

31. *The 8th Habit*, 5.

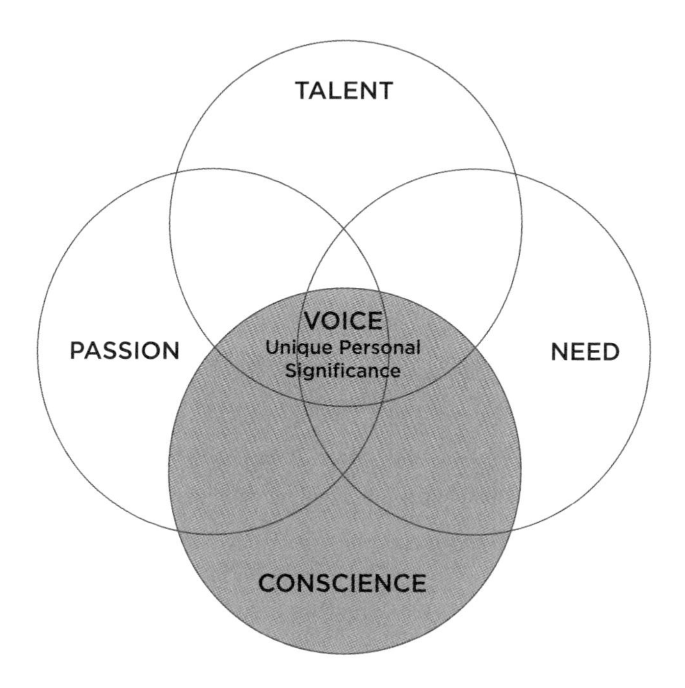

There is a deep, innate, almost inexpressible yearning within each one of us to find our voice in life. It's wrapped up in our identity and self-respect. It's not just the talent or passion that surges to the fore without external incentives, nor is it just the urgings of conscience, although these are essential to the voice. It's also knowing that we are needed, that the world values the uniqueness in us.

There is a deep, innate, almost inexpressible yearning within each one of us to find our voice in life.

In other words, an engaging mission must appeal to people's passionate interests, leverage their distinctive talents, satisfy the conscience, and meet a compelling market need. It's not easy to fulfill all of these criteria at the same time, but the leader's job is to combine all those elements of the organization's "voice." Leaders who do so tap into a miraculous power source.

Begin now to evaluate the mission of your team or organization:

- ***Talent***. Are you leveraging the irreplaceable talents of team members? Do you even know what they are?
- ***Passion***. Is everyone passionate about that job? Do they come at it with energy and determination, or do they just go through the motions?
- ***Conscience***. Are you meeting the demands of conscience? Is your organization doing what it should do? Are you tapping into people's innate desire to be socially responsible?
- ***Need***. What is the specific job your customers are hiring you to do? Have you really answered that question? The job you are being hired to do is very different

> than a job description. It requires careful stakeholder analysis. What are they trying to achieve through your contribution? What are they willing to PAY for? Are you in sync with the needs of an ever-evolving market? Are you staying on top of market hot spots, or are they moving away from you?

What you are really doing here is telling your team story. What anecdotes do you tell about your own successes? your failures? What is exciting about the job you do? How could you raise the bar on excitement and involvement? Imagine your mission statement as a lead story in the news. What would be the headline? What would make the story viral?

One team that clearly found its voice—and benefited others in significant ways by doing so—is part of the U.S. Army Medical Research and Material Command (MRMC). MRMC's mission is to: "Responsively and responsibly create, develop, deliver, and sustain medical capabilities for the Warfighter." Jacques Reifman, a senior research scientist with the U.S. Army, found his voice within this mission. Reifman "argued for years that we measure the vital signs, but that we don't know if the data we are collecting is actually information we need to be sure someone is in critical condition."[32] But this team's mission was broader than simply providing vital signs. It was about sustaining

32. Partnership for Public Service, "Samuel J. Heyman Service to America Medals 2016 Winner: Science and Environment." Undated. https://servicetoamericamedals.org/honorees/view_profile.php?profile=443

medical capabilities for the Warfighter. It was about truly helping medical personnel in combat.

Reifman knew that approximately 22 percent of Iraq- and Afghanistan-conflict casualties who died after severe bleeding could actually have been saved.[33] What did Reifman do to confront this issue?

He led a team of passionate and talented engineers, medical technicians, and software developers to create the Automated Processing of the Physiologic Registry for Assessment of Injury Severity system, or APPRAISE. APPRAISE uses an off-the-shelf vital-signs monitor and a ruggedized PC to create "an artificial intelligence system for medics to quickly detect if severely injured patients in transit are hemorrhaging, improving survival rates by preparing trauma centers to act immediately upon the patient's arrival."

Boston MedFlight started testing APPRAISE in 2010. They found the system capable of identifying—within under ten minutes—75 to 80 percent of patients with life-threatening internal bleeding whose issues otherwise would not have been detected. This paved "the way for Boston-area trauma units to be ready for immediate surgery and replenishment of lost blood, without wasting time and

33. Lori A. DeBernardis and Anna K. Applegate, "BHSAI Develops System to Identify Patients with Severe Bleeding During Transport," USMRMC, April 14, 2015. http://mrmc.amedd.army.mil/index.cfm?pageid=media_resources.articles.BHSAI_develops_system_to_identify_patients_with_severe_bleeding

resources on false alarms." Reifman's alignment to MRMC's mission helps not only patients in Boston, but civilian and military personnel worldwide.

"Not too often do scientists have an idea or a dream, and then over time advance the science to take the concept to deployment and show how it works," Reifman said. MRMC's mission and continued support allowed Reifman's dream to become a reality.

You can see that the mission of MRMC is far more engaging than you'll find in the vast majority of "organizational mission statements."

MRMC engages the talents and passions of its people by valuing those talents and passions *above all else*.

Again, what about your mission? Are you truly engaging the talent, passion, *and* conscience of people in meeting needs that matter?

Get Aligned to the Mission

What's the second reason people are cynical about the typical mission statement? The organization is too often misaligned with it. The grand pronouncements on the bronze plaque don't line up with the things people are asked to do every day (or what they see their leaders modeling). In short, managers don't walk the talk. It doesn't matter how fervid the language. If the mission statement is about "valuing those we serve above all" while management obsesses over everything *but* the people it serves, employees will simply disengage from the mission. They will naturally ask, "If it doesn't matter to the front office, why should it matter to me?"

Assuming you really want people to engage with the mission, everything you do needs to align to it. This means carefully examining (and redesigning, if necessary) the core processes of the organization—everything from strategy to operations to policy to support. Are any of these processes undermining the mission?

Every core process needs to support the mission in a simple, visible, and consistent way.

Think of the core process in the dabbawala organization. After collecting the lunchboxes between 9:00 and 10:00 in the morning, the dabbawalas pack them onto trolleys and push them to the railway station. The boxes go by train to a central station for unloading. Each box is color-coded so that those going to similar destinations end up on the same trolley. A given lunchbox might pass through the hands of four different dabbawalas before it arrives at its destination by 12:30 p.m. At the receiving station, the dabbawalas load the boxes onto their trademark silver bicycles. The dabbawalas have only their bicycles, the coded boxes, and the city train system as resources to navigate through one of the largest, most crowded, most complicated cities in the world.

Every core process needs to support the mission in a simple, visible, and consistent way.

In the afternoon, they reverse the process, picking up the empty boxes and returning them to the residents. That's more than 400,000 nearly mistake-free transactions every single day—for more than a century.

Because the dabbawalas' system of "carrying the curry" is virtually perfect, it has attracted the attention of Harvard Business School, *The Economist* magazine, the ISO 9000 authority of Australia, and even the Prince of Wales.[34] Scholars and students of supply-chain management are amazed. After studying the dabbawalas' system, *Forbes* magazine writers compared it to a Six Sigma process, which means the lunchbox men make only one error in every 16 million transactions! How do they do it? As *Forbes* asked, "How can a system based on barefoot men, public trains,

34. Paul S. Goodman, "The Cult of the Dabbawala," *The Economist*, July 10, 2008. http://www.economist.com/node/11707779

and simple, reusable containers" be one of the top core processes in the world?[35]

According to the professionals who evaluated it, the dabbawalas' process works so well because it is *simple, visible,* and *consistent.*

Everyone, from the youngest dabbawala to the chairman of the association, can describe the process. The dabbawalas know exactly where they are going 100 percent of the time.

The system is *visible.* The lunchbox code contains the entire work process from start to finish. A few symbols on each lid indicate exactly where the lunchbox came from and where it is going. For example, a box picked up at Vile Parle railway station routes through Churchgate Station—we know this from the symbol of a cross on the lid. Then it moves on to a particular building indicated by blue lettering. The numbers "1–2" communicate the endpoint: the second office on the first floor.

And *consistency* is, of course, the hallmark of the dabbawalas' service. You can count on them without question. The dabbawalas take pride in their consistent quality of service. They wear distinctive white caps and tunics, and their

35. Karl Moore, "The Best Way to Innovation? An Important Lesson from India," *Forbes*, May 24, 2011. http://www.forbes.com/sites/karlmoore/2011/05/24/the-best-way-to-innovation-an-important-lesson-from-india/; Sue Gillman, "4 Reasons the Dabbawala Supply Chain Succeeds While Corporate Giants Struggle," I Six Sigma, July 8, 2011. http://www.isixsigma.com/community/blogs/4-reasons-dabbawala-supply-chain-succeeds-while-corporate-giants-struggle/

silver bicycles are recognized everywhere. There is no overreliance on technology, but there is a lot of reliance on a winning team.

The passion of the dabbawalas means they never let down a customer. When a disastrous monsoon struck Mumbai in 2005, many thousands of people drowned or were lost. The city's massive network of trains, which the dabbawalas depend on, stopped completely. So the dabbawalas left the trains and made their way several kilometers to their checkpoints on foot, carrying the dabbas through the torrential rains and floods. Few if any customers were missed. Uninterrupted service is that important to the dabbawalas.

Of course, as the world changes, the dabbawalas change too. That's why they are now taking orders by text and expanding their services. For example, their clockwork precision and custom delivery makes them an attractive distribution outlet for everything from time-sensitive software advertisements to investment brochures. As one dabbawala says, "There is a service called FedEx that is similar to ours—but they don't deliver lunch."[36] Through it all, the core process stays simple, transparent, and utterly reliable. Every single day, battling the vast crowds of Mumbai,

---

36. Saritha Rai, "In India, Grandma Cooks, They Deliver," *The New York Times*, May 29, 2007. http://www.nytimes.com/2007/05/29/business/worldbusiness/29lunch.html?pagewanted=1&_r=1]

unbelievable heat, or monsoon floods, the dabbawalas serve their customers with calm consistency.

Paul S. Goodman of Carnegie-Mellon University observes, "Most of our modern business education is about analytic models, technology and efficient business practices. The dabbawalas, by contrast, focus more on human and social ingenuity."[37] They focus on the people, on the pride of being unique, on the strength of commitment to the mission.

What about your core processes? Are they…

- Simple?
- Visible?
- Consistent?

What could you do to simplify your processes? Make them more visible? Make them more consistent with the mission of the organization and consistent in execution?

In the end, people will never engage with a "mission" that is not a mission, that is meaningless organization-speak. And if they're not asked to live by it, the mission doesn't matter anyway.

37. Goodman, "The Cult of the Dabbawala."

People will never engage with a "mission" that is not a mission, that is meaningless organization-speak.

But if you want to engage the full power of your people, involve them in finding your organization's voice, then let that voice govern everything you do.

Leading With Purpose: Instructions for Downloading

Here are key steps to lead your team or organization with purpose. Involve your team in discussing these *questions*. The outcomes should be (1) an *engaging* mission statement and (2) core processes that clearly support that mission.

Step	Discussion Points
Find the voice of your team.	• Do we have a written team mission? Are we passionate about our team mission? Does it inspire our energy and determination, or are we just going through the motions? • Does our mission leverage the irreplaceable talents of each team member? Do we even know what they are? • Does our mission meet the demands of conscience? Are we doing what we should do? Are we socially responsible? - What is the specific job our customers are hiring us to do? Is it changing? - Who are our most important customers? - What are their most important goals? - What unique capabilities do we bring to help them meet those goals? • Given our answers to these questions, how can we refine our mission statement?
Get aligned to the mission.	• What are our core processes? • Do our core processes clearly support the mission? • What do we need to do make our core processes: - Simple? - Visible? - Consistent?

CHAPTER 6

PRACTICE 2: EXECUTE WITH EXCELLENCE

DISCIPLINE IS THE HALLMARK OF SUCCESSFUL INDIVIDUALS AND ORGANIZATIONS

-

"A feeble execution is but another phrase for a bad execution; and a government ill executed, what may be its theory, must, in practice be a bad government."

–Judge Joseph Story

-

People with a mission are the most engaged people. When they are actually achieving their mission, they are *doubly* engaged. It's one thing to have a mission; it's quite another to execute it. Many people join public-sector organizations because they are passionate about the mission. They want to find housing for the homeless, protect and defend the homeland, ensure that the needs of local citizens are met, and a litany of other important and worthy work; however, they often become disenfranchised when they see that the goals they want to accomplish never seem to happen. As

Stephen R. Covey said, "People are caught up in the thick of thin things"; the mission somehow gets lost along the way.

As a government leader, you may have identified a compelling and well-constructed strategy for carrying out the mission, but no matter how visionary you are, you can't truly be a leader unless you produce results. Fulfilling that strategy requires a deeply engaged team. Creating that team is the leader's perennial challenge.

Have you ever spent a day in a conference room with your team brainstorming goals for the coming fiscal year? If so, you know how challenging that process can be. Someone stands with marker in hand and fills up large pieces of paper with team-member ideas. The team then hangs the sheets on the wall, and everyone agrees: "This is what we're going to do." Six months later, you discover the papers rolled up and stuck behind the file cabinet in your office. Or perhaps you have been involved in a strategic planning process for your organization. You invested time to listen to your stakeholders, assess the organization, craft a vision for the future, and ultimately produce a strategic plan with your organization's name (probably in an acronymesque format) emblazoned across the front of it. The document looks great. The plan is sound. However, for some reason, the grand ideas don't come to fruition.

Consider this: How often have you heard leaders announce a bold new initiative, only to watch the initiative die a slow, painful death? Most strategies fail, not because they are poor strategies, but because they are never executed.

Most strategies fail, not because they are poor strategies, but because they are never executed.

Discouragement reigns when a team member becomes inspired and motivated about a big change and then nothing changes. In one case, the leaders of a government agency announced a major change in direction. A new leader was brought in to lead the "transformation." Presentations were made, logos were added to email signature blocks, and posters went up on the wall. People were excited, but they went back to work the next day and didn't hear much about it after that. Occasionally, someone would ask, "Whatever happened to that great new program?" The team slowly—but surely—disengaged. But at least they had the posters.

Meanwhile, the leaders were frustrated by the lack of progress on the initiative. They held special meetings to discuss why the program was not gaining traction. People nodded their heads and agreed to double down on their efforts to get things moving. Then they went back to work and the initiative was again forgotten. Eighteen months later, the senior leader changed jobs and everyone stopped talking about it altogether—it was too embarrassing.

This scenario might be extreme, but it's not uncommon. We can point to examples in nearly every government organization where this experience has occurred. Most can point to at least one example (perhaps many?) where a carefully designed and very important strategy has gathered dust for lack of execution.

Occasionally, there's resistance to a strategy. Sometimes people cross their arms and suggest the leader who dreamed up this idea won't be here forever. We call this the "we can wait the leader out" syndrome. Perhaps people resist because they fear that moving in a new direction will cause them to lose power, take on too much new work, or head down a path they watched fail in the past.

From our experience, however, the most common reason for strategic failure—by far—is a lack of organizational focus. Think about it: the leaders give you a new program, a new goal, a new strategy; but your day-to-day work doesn't go away, so you can't give it enough focus. You have to keep doing what you've been doing (remember the mantra of "more with less") and meet the new goal as well. You've got to "get back to work." In addition, by asking you to do something new, the leaders are asking you to do something you've never done before. They're asking you to change your behavior, which is the hardest thing anyone ever tries to do. Think about it: how difficult is it to change your own behavior? How about changing the behavior of another? Or even more daunting, changing the behavior of a whole bunch of people in order to achieve a new goal? Whether you're trying to lose weight, play the piano, win at golf, or execute a strategic goal with excellence, sustained success requires extraordinary commitment.

Whether you're trying to lose weight, play the piano, win at golf, or execute a strategic goal with excellence, sustained success requires extraordinary commitment.

We call the day-to-day work the "whirlwind." And the whirlwind is critical. In most cases, workers can't simply walk away from it. It is required just to keep the lights on. So how in the world can one be expected to execute something new, especially when new behaviors are required?

The State of Georgia's former commissioner of human services, B.J. Walker, led her 9,000-person department for seven years and guided them to accomplish significant goals. From 2004 to 2011, she oversaw efforts leading to the reduction of adults on welfare from 27,192 to only

2,297. Of those who remained on rolls, 68 percent of them performed work activities for at least 30 hours per week. Additionally, B.J.'s department reduced the incidents of child maltreatment from 9.2 percent to 2.54 percent as compared to a nationwide average of 5.4 percent, and the state of Georgia went from last in the nation to among the top five states in its success in transitioning developmentally disabled people from state institutions to community-based programs. In talking about her experience, B.J. summed up the challenge of executing a goal in the midst of the daily "whirlwind" by suggesting that "the reason why people struggle with execution is because they have no process… week to week, day to day…to get from where they are to where they want to go."[38]

You see, it's no longer enough to have a great strategy. The job to be done now is to get yourself and your team absolutely clear on the Wildly Important Goals and discipline yourselves to execute with excellence and precision.

The job used to be...	The job you must do now...
Come up with a great strategy.	Execute your strategy with excellence and precision to get the results you need to achieve.

How do you do this? How do you accomplish the behavior change required to execute in the midst of an

38. "State of Georgia Department of Health and Human Services." *4DX Video Case Study*. FranklinCovey Company, 2008.

unrelenting whirlwind? There is both good news and bad news as it relates to this question.

The good news is that there are rules for executing in the midst of the whirlwind—four of them, in fact. We call them *The 4 Disciplines of Execution®*. If followed, they will empower and engage a team to new and better behaviors. They will clarify the critical goals, behaviors, and commitments required for success.

The bad news is there are rules for executing in the midst of the whirlwind. You can ignore them, but they won't ignore you. And each of them is counterintuitive to what we might normally do. So they require particular attention.

The 4 Disciplines of Execution

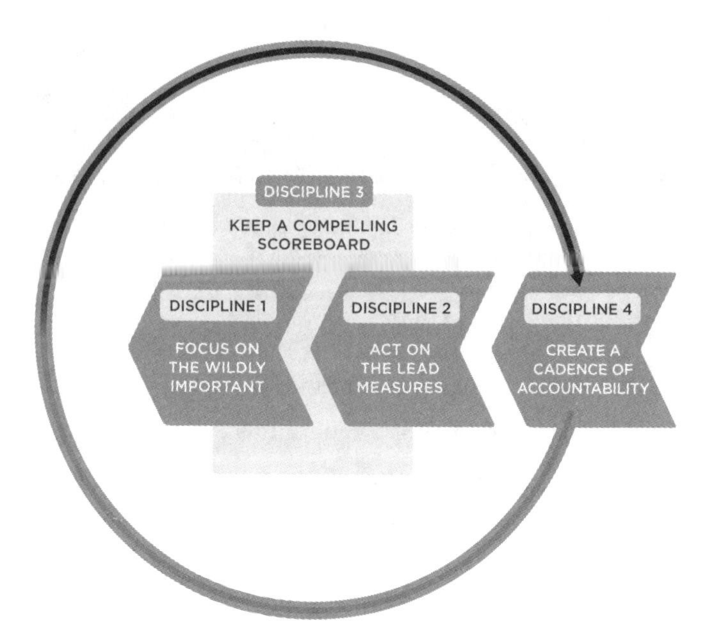

Here are the 4 Disciplines of Execution with excellence[39]:

1. Focus on the Wildly Important
2. Act on the Lead Measures
3. Keep a Compelling Scoreboard
4. Create a Cadence of Accountability

39. Chris McChesney, Sean Covey, Jim Huling, *The 4 Disciplines of Execution*, New York City: Simon & Schuster, 2012.

Discipline 1: Focus on the Wildly Important

Most people are trying to do too much. To stay engaged in the real priorities, leaders need to be careful to distinguish what is merely "important" from what is "wildly important." A goal that is wildly important is one that has a gap that needs to be closed and will, therefore, receive the organization's best diligence and effort. It's a goal that, if not accomplished, renders everything else inconsequential. Because human beings have limits, we can usually reach one goal with excellence. But if we have much more than this, it stands to reason we'll do half a job on each. Consider the following chart. If your team has two to three clearly defined goals, chances are pretty good that the team can accomplish two to three. Ask us to reach five, six, ten, or more goals and our chances of executing them all with excellence are nil. This is our version of the "law of diminishing returns."

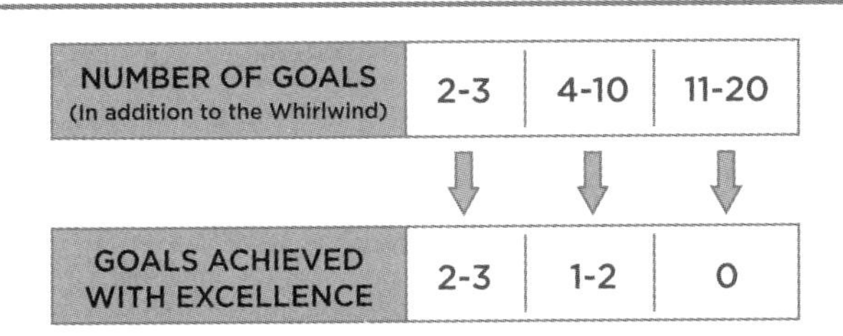

Your chances of achieving 2 or 3 goals with excellence are high, but the more goals you try to juggle at once, the less likely you will be to reach them.

A goal that is wildly important is one that has a gap that must be closed and will, therefore, receive the organization's best diligence and effort.

It sounds obvious, but organizations have a way of piling up "must do" priorities, making it impossible to do a very good job on any of them. Here is where the first discipline is counterintuitive. We become overwhelmed in priorities because organizations are filled with smart, capable people who have lots of genuinely good ideas—ideas that, if executed, will make a difference. Discipline 1 requires leaders to say no to good ideas.

A key recipe for disengaging people is to overwhelm them with things to do, all of which are "Job 1" and "key priorities" and "top of the list." But if you unleash people to focus on just one, two, or three Wildly Important Goals® (WIGs)—no more—they will sense the significance of what they're doing and they'll have a chance to win. There is tremendous power in focus. As you prioritize your goals, think about those things that must be done, and if not done, nothing else matters. Focus on those true priorities, and move lower priorities to the back burner. Government organizations are hierarchical in nature, and that structure often compounds the lack-of-focus problem.

In these organizations, when the senior leader says, "That's a good idea," people immediately assume it must be done and another goal, initiative, or project is added to the stack.

There is tremendous power in focus.

Be sure to establish a clear and shared understanding of the goal. Leaders often assume the objective is understood by everyone, when there's usually wide and divergent understanding. Lawrence Hrebiniak reports, "I've done consulting where a major strategic thrust has been developed, and a month or two later I go down four or five levels and ask people how they're doing. They haven't even heard of the program."[40] B.J. Walker echoes Hrebiniak's assertion. Talking about the challenge of getting her 9,000 employees clear on an overarching goal, she said "Everybody knows we have a Wildly Important Goal. They know it's about death and serious injury and they know we are trying to reduce. For a giant bureaucratic organization, anybody in the government will tell you, if everybody in your organization knows that much about something you are doing, that's a miracle."

40. "Three Reasons Why Good Strategies Fail." August, 2015. Wharton College, University of Pennsylvania

We met once with a group of senior government leaders—the executive team for a newly formed agency with a new mandate. They had already worked for days creating their strategic plan when we met with them, so we conducted a little experiment. We asked each one separately to tell us the agency's top priorities and key goals. We were fascinated by the responses—they were all over the map! Every single person had a different idea of what was wildly important, even though after days of planning, they had assumed they were all on the same page.

If a goal is wildly important, it's worth being precise about it. That means you should formulate it in terms of where you are now (X), where you want to be (Y), and when will you accomplish it. In other words, "From X to Y by When." For example, it's not enough to have a goal to "lose weight." You need to express it as, say, "Reduce my weight from 195 lbs. to 180 lbs. by June 1." Now you have a starting line, a finish line, and a deadline. It will be easy to tell if you achieve your goal or not.

In 1958, the U.S. space program was significantly behind the Soviet Union's program. America's goal was to "maximize our effectiveness in space." On another occasion, the mandate was "to lead the world in space exploration"; nothing specific, nothing measurable, something of a yawn. Then, on May 5, 1961, in a speech before a joint session of Congress, President John F. Kennedy proposed the goal "to send a man to the moon and return him safely to the earth by the end of the decade." This Wildly Important Goal, "From the earth to the moon and back by 1970," engaged and energized the entire nation. It was achieved.

If a goal is wildly important and people know it matters most, their engagement goes off the charts—in fact, it's tough to distract them. Formula One race-car drivers don't answer their cell phones during the race.

When Tom Weisner became mayor of Aurora, the largest city in Illinois after Chicago, he confronted dozens of important issues: The Fox River district was blighted; the crime rate was sky-high; gang violence had reached a high point with 26 murders the prior year; scores of businesses had fled the city, leaving an unemployment problem; and city workers weren't even taking down the annual holiday decorations. (This last issue was a really sore point with a lot of people.) With so much on his plate, Mayor Weisner could have tried to "eat it all," but he didn't. He wisely surveyed his entire team of 1,200 workers in choosing no more than three Wildly Important Goals. They would decide together what those three were.

Since no one had ever asked them before, the city workers had plenty of ideas. After repeated discussions with them and other civic groups, the city leaders chose three Wildly Important Goals for the year:

1. Reduce shootings by 20 percent.
2. Reduce the resolution time for citizen requests from all city divisions by 20 percent.
3. Revitalize the Fox River Corridor by approving a minimum of 650 new residential units and create one acre of open space for the corridor.

Everyone agreed that if the first goal was not met, nothing else would matter very much. The image of a dangerous city was wrecking everything. The second goal meant a lot to the citizens; to catch up on a huge backlog of requests would rekindle their faith in the city. The third goal was about turning a declining city into a revitalized city. These goals were "wildly important" to everyone's future, and the people who *set* the goals *owned* them. They were engaged.

Once you have set clear Wildly Important Goals, it's time to define everyone's role in achieving them. Each person must consider, "How do *I* contribute to achieving the goals?" Unless they all know the answer to that question, they will disengage.

Discipline 2: Act on the Lead Measures

In tracking progress on a goal, there are two kinds of measures: lead and lag. The lead measures track actions you set and take to achieve the goal. For example, consuming fewer calories each day and exercising regularly will lead to weight loss (as long as the laws of physics remain in place). Therefore, the lead measures for weight loss are the number of calories consumed and the number of calories burned each day. The lag measures quantify the results. For example, if your goal is to lose weight, the lag measure is what the scale tells you about your progress. This is the counterintuitive behavior associated with this discipline: managing lead measures instead of just lag measures. Tracking lead measures is harder than tracking the lag measure, but you will do it if you're serious about your goal. Unless you hit the lead measures, you will probably not hit the lag measure.

The task is to select a few lead measures that have the most impact on the lag measure. You could make the mistake of selecting lead measures that make little or no difference. You could give up eating pastries, for example, but if you don't limit your overall calorie intake, that action alone won't matter much. Or you might choose a lead measure you can't control, such as getting the organization's cafeteria to change its menu. To effectively reach your goals, personally or organizationally, you must choose lead measures you can control and that will make a true difference in the outcome. Lead measures must be both predictive to and have influence on the desired outcome. As our team worked with Mayor Weisner and his team, it became very clear that cutting the murder rate was top of the list for the city of Aurora. The lead measure the city workers adopted was to break up drug gangs by getting the gang leaders off the streets. Within months, the police had swept the city clean of 21 gang leaders. As for the third goal, revitalizing the Fox River district would require new, more attractive space for businesses and residents. City leaders set a lead measure to talk with 50 developers about new construction in Aurora. By the end of the year, they had exceeded their goal and had 95 actively interested developers.

Determining Lead Measures

How do you decide which lead measures to work on? Here, the expertise of the team comes in. The people on the front line probably know more about what actually moves the business than anyone else. The City of Aurora realized that reducing the murder rate was not the sole responsibility of the police force; other departments could also play a role in achieving this goal. Municipal workers knew that crimes usually happened in poorly lit areas, so their lead measure was to ensure that all burned-out city lights were replaced within three hours. They also knew that crimes tended to occur where graffiti had been painted, so they established a "remove graffiti within twenty-four hours" rule as a second lead measure. These are just two examples. Each department created its own lead measures toward achieveing the ultimate goal.

The takeaway is to get the team to define the lead measures. Call on their knowledge and their creativity and watch them get fully engaged. It's also important to hold them accountable to the lead measures—they are responsible to act on those. Thinking back to the losing-weight example, what do you have control over—what you eat and if you exercise, or what number the scale shows? Unless you're manipulating the dial on the scale, it's the former. In the same way, you will disengage your people if you call them constantly on the lag measures—"Why are we having so many safety issues?" "Why is the crime rate still going up?" "Why is fundraising down so much this year?" That is not leadership. The secret to achieving Wildly Important Goals is *not* to set them and then hope people will somehow get them done. Instead, true leaders work with people to decide which lead measures are within their power and then hold them accountable for acting on those lead measures. People engage when they know they can actually make a difference.

True leaders work with people to decide which lead measures are within their power and then hold them accountable for acting on those lead measures.

Discipline 3: Keep a Compelling Scoreboard

Shawn tells this story: "When I lived in Philadelphia, I liked to go down the street to the playground in my inner-city neighborhood and play basketball with the neighbors' kids. It was fun to try to match skills. Usually, we just fooled around with the ball, but sometimes we kept score. As soon as we started playing for points, something happened on the court: all of a sudden, the intensity level went up. Eyes narrowed, sweat poured, signals flew hard and fast, cooperation increased, an audience gathered to cheer and groan. As long as we were just playing around, everything was mellow, but when we knew the score, things got serious. *We were engaged.*"

Like the neighborhood basketball players in Philadelphia, people are energized by "the score." Everything changes when you're keeping score—when you know if you're winning or losing. You need a scoreboard so you can tell at a glance how things are going. The people in Aurora got excited when they saw they could "move the needle" on the Crime-Rate Scoreboard. As it started dropping, they became more engaged and more creative about moving it even more.

That's why it's crucial to keep a compelling scoreboard—a simple picture with only a few numbers on it. "We already have plenty of scoreboards," you say. "We have numbers coming out of our ears." But we're not talking about the vast compilations of data your organization tracks. Although those numbers have their place, we're talking about the numbers that are wildly important: the lag and lead measures on the Wildly Important Goals. All we need to see is the lag measure—"Is the murder rate dropping?"—and the lead measure—"How many gang leaders have we cleared off the streets?" These numbers tell us if we're making a difference or not.

Here is what's counterintuitive about this discipline: this is not a *coach's* scoreboard. It is a *players'* scoreboard, created by the players.

We once toured a large aircraft factory where thousands of workers were divided into small groups, each focused on making one part of an airplane. At each of these work stations, a computer monitor displayed huge amounts of data in tiny fonts. If you really studied these displays—*really* studied them—you could figure out what the numbers meant. We asked the teams why the monitors were there.

Most of them didn't know and the ones who did said they never took time to look at them.

So we asked the managers, "Why all the complicated data displays all over the factory?" They responded, "We want work groups to be able to see the impact they're making on the production process." They'd missed their mark. Imagine watching a sporting event on TV—a football match or a basketball game—with every single statistic related to the event displayed on the screen but no way to see the score! That was the situation in the factory.

Imagine watching a sporting event on TV—a football match or a basketball game—with every single statistic related to the event displayed on the screen but no way to see the score!

By contrast, one of our clients, a military training facility, posts large scoreboards with just a few numbers and images showing the rate of progress toward the Wildly Important Goals. But that's not all—each team member can tell, within three seconds of looking at the scoreboard, if they are hitting their lead measures and if they will deliver on their goal. One employee told us, "We've talked for years about accomplishing this goal, but it never seems to happen.

Now, I can look at the board; we all can look at the board and see our progress. We are going to do it this time."

The scoreboard is for the team, not just the leaders. That's why it needs to be big and visible and constantly updated. People play differently when *they're* keeping score. Chris McChesney, FranklinCovey's global Execution practice leader, sums up the power of the scoreboard: "The highest level of performance always comes from people who are emotionally engaged, and the highest level of engagement comes from knowing the score; that is, knowing whether one is winning or losing. If your team members don't know whether they are winning the game, they are probably on their way to losing."[41]

People play differently when they're keeping score.

When teams start to build their own scoreboards, leaders can become a bit concerned. They sometimes ask, *Is it okay that these look so unsophisticated? Shouldn't we have an elaborate device to show the importance of these metrics?* Or, *What will senior leadership think when they see these "homemade"-looking scoreboards?*

41. Chris McChesney, Jim Huling, "Four Reasons Why Your Strategy Will Fail (And What to Do About It)," *Forbes*, Jan. 25, 2013. http://www.forbes.com/sites/forbesleadershipforum/2013/01/25/four-reasons-why-your-2013-strategy-will-fail/

Patrick tells the story of a pharmaceutical company that went through the *4 Disciplines* process. "The organization did an absolutely incredible job accomplishing its goals. They surpassed all expectations and the teams were very excited. One morning I received a call from my client informing me that a new executive had joined the organization and would serve as my client's new leader. The person on the other end of the phone expressed concern that new leader might react negatively to the team scoreboards. After all, the team scoreboards depicted caterpillars and butterflies to demonstrate the team's transformation."

Alex Azar was that incoming executive. A Yale-educated attorney, Alex had received a political appointment and served as the Deputy Director of the U.S. Department of Health and Human Services. Prior to that role, he worked as the HHS General Counsel. Patrick explains, "My client was concerned that a former deputy director at an agency with tens of thousands of employees might have an aversion to the simple team scoreboard. He asked me questions like, 'Wouldn't a leader coming from an organization of tens of thousands of employees expect a more sophisticated system? Wouldn't he expect to see a leader's scoreboard?' My response was simply to not borrow trouble and allow the teams to show what they'd accomplished. Perhaps we would focus more on the results and less on the displays."

The meeting went extremely well. The results were tremendous, the teams engaged, and the leader impressed. But don't take our word for it. A couple of years later, we received this letter from Alex Azar.

> "When I saw a three-hour meeting on my calendar that day, I was skeptical. As a new VP of Eli Lilly and Company's U.S. affiliate, I was swamped. But since one of my leaders was running the meeting, I decided to attend.
>
> "It was a decision I will always be glad I made, because within the first few minutes of the meeting, I realized I was seeing something special. I watched a team reporting on the remarkable results they had achieved by piloting a new set of practices known as *The 4 Disciplines of Execution.* These were individuals who had not only achieved their goals, but who walked and talked like *winners*. Their chests were out and their heads held high. As a leader, I wanted those results, but more important, I wanted that *mindset* throughout my entire organization.
>
> "We launched *The 4 Disciplines* throughout our managed healthcare business, aiming at two critical goals: to dramatically increase customer access to our medicines while simultaneously improving bottom-line profitability. During the same period, there was a larger initiative throughout Lilly to reorganize for more effective

operations. We could not have chosen a more difficult context for creating engagement. In the end, we exceeded both of our goals by a significant margin, but these results were not really our greatest outcome.

"Our greatest outcome was strengthening our culture by raising the engagement of our teams. During a time of high demand coupled with a reorganization that brought significant change, our employee-engagement scores actually *went up*.

"I often look back on the decision to attend the initial meeting, and more important, on the journey we've made to create not only great business results but also a high-performing culture. I was a pivotal decision for me—one that changed the way I lead forever.

Alex Azar
President, Lilly USA, LLC"

Obviously, the scoreboard is a simple device that gives strategy execution something of the quality of a game. But it has a very serious purpose. Professor Hrebiniak reports that fewer than 15 percent of organizations routinely track their strategic performance against their plan. In other words, hardly anybody is keeping score.[42] Is it any wonder then that so many work teams, having no idea what the score is, are profoundly disengaged? The scoreboard enables people to track activities, compare results, and improve performance continuously. By watching the scoreboard closely, they can tell if their lead measures are well chosen. Are the lead measures actually having an effect on the lag measures? If not, it's time to rethink. By watching the few scores that matter very closely, the team can change strategy if needed. That's what an engaged team does.

Keeping It Going

So, what if you get everyone together and decide on the Wildly Important Goals? You set your measures, you put up your scoreboard, and then watch the whole thing die.

This could happen, unless you add the next level of accountability. This is why: people will be excited at first. They will embrace the new goal because they've helped make it. They will commit to the new behaviors (lead measures) necessary to achieve the goal. The scoreboard will give them focus. But they need momentum to get it going. Unless the team comes together *regularly* and *often* to gauge progress, team members will disengage and wonder what happened to that goal. If you plan to drive from New York

42. "Three Reasons."

to California, you don't just fill your car up once with gas and expect to make it all the way there. You start out making good progress, but eventually, you're going to need to fill up again. In the same way, you need to fill your workers' "tanks" by holding them accountable and reigniting their enthusiasm as they see how far they've come.

But how do you do that?

A Colorado business professor, Wayne Boss, got interested in what he called the "regression effect," the tendency of work teams to get really enthusiastic about new goals and strategies and then gradually disengage. Boss is a student of team dynamics, so he spent a lot of time watching teams come together, make plans, get fired up, and then forget the whole thing. He had watched organizations do everything they could think of to psych up the workers about a new initiative: big parties, loud music, rap videos, giveaway programs, celebrity appearances, even clown mascots running through the aisles. Most people enjoyed these events and went away fired up, but their behavior did not change. As Boss puts it, they invariably regressed: "During a two- or three-day intensive team-building activity, people became very enthusiastic about making improvements, but within a few weeks, the spark dwindles, and they regress to old behaviors and performance levels."

Boss experimented with many ways to keep engagement high. By far, the most effective was to just meet regularly and monitor progress often. We call it a "cadence of accountability." Cadence is a "balanced, rhythmic flow" of activity, like a cycle that repeats itself.

If your team goal is in fact wildly important, you can't afford not to have a cadence of accountability.

Discipline 4: Create a Cadence of Accountability

The cadence of accountability is a simple four-step process that will help you and the team you lead cut through the clutter and chaos of the day-to-day grind and engage in your department's or organization's Wildly Important Goals.

Here's how the cadence works.

First of all, make sure everyone on the team can influence the goal. The goal defines the team. Don't include people who can't "move the needle" on the scoreboard. In your first meeting, make sure everyone's role in achieving the goal is clearly defined. (You may want to do this in a private one-on-one meeting.) Practice the highly effective habit of first listening to understand. Get each team member's perspective. Ask, "What do you want to contribute?" then give your own perspective. Be synergistic and merge into an agreement. The counterintuitive behavior with this discipline is that the leader can't tell the people what to do—even if they're used to it or if they ask you to do it.

Boss describes this role negotiation this way: "[The leader and the team member] clarify their expectations of each other, what they need from each other, and what they will contract to do." Stephen R. Covey called this contract a "Win-Win Agreement," in which all parties define what their "wins" are.

Then meet with the whole team at least weekly (after all, we're talking about a Wildly Important Goal) to check progress. If you don't meet for two, three, or more weeks, team members *will* disengage from the goal in the midst of everything else they have to do. This meeting is *not* your staff meeting; its sole purpose is to move the goal forward.

The agenda of the meeting is simple. Start by reviewing the scoreboard. Is the lag measure moving in the right direction? Are the lead measures having any effect? Are we where we're supposed to be or have we slipped behind? Should we reconsider our lead measures?

Then review the agreements, the things each team member committed to do the prior week. Celebrate successes; help people who are running into barriers. This is the value of a complementary team: if a team member encounters an obstacle, other team members might be able to help remove it. The leader, in particular, can do things no one else can, such as getting access to resources and talking to senior leaders.

Then make new commitments for the next week. What's the one thing each team member can do that will have the most impact on the measures? These commitments are recorded and shared and form the agenda for the next meeting. Keeping your commitments to your team can engage you more than anything else.

After studying hundreds of teams over a decade, Boss found that if these meetings are held on a regular basis (weekly, biweekly, or monthly) and follow the agreed-upon agenda, performance can stay high without regression for several years. "Without exception...group effectiveness was maintained only in those teams that employed [the process], while the teams that did not use it evidenced regression in the months after their team-building session."[43]

Boss also found that the cadence of accountability is "most effective when conducted in a climate of high support and trust. Establishing this climate is primarily the responsibility of the [leader]." He explained that leaders must be ready to ask the difficult "why" questions if tasks are not completed, but they must do so with the attitude of helping to "clear the path."

With the cadence of accountability, team members get the support and feedback they yearn for. More than 60 percent of employees—especially the twenty-eight-and-under millennials—say they don't get enough feedback. Many managers give feedback only once a year at performance-appraisal time. That's like a basketball coach telling the players at the beginning of the season, "You're going to go out and play thirty games, and at the end of the season,

43. W. Gibb Dyer, et al., *Team Building: Proven Strategies for Improving Performance*, John Wiley & Sons, 2013, 120–121.

I'll evaluate your performance." Frequent feedback relates directly to performance.

In speaking about the cadence of accountability in Georgia's Department of Human Services, B.J. Walker put it this way, "Who likes another meeting in government? Name them. But then you look at the engagement of the people, it's incredible." B.J. Walker saw the power of involvement, commitment, and accountability to drive employee engagement.

By following these principles and this process, you will do more to create a highly engaged, self-starting team than anything else you can do.

The 4 Disciplines and Team Engagement

Now, what happened to the city workers in Aurora, Illinois, as they started to live by the principles of excellent execution? "The city missed its first goal—shootings were reduced by 14.5 percent, rather than 20 percent—but the following two goals were achieved. Only a few departments fell short of the 20 percent reduction in response time, and the two big development agreements for projects on either side of the river exceeded the goal for residential units and open space." Additionally, murders dropped from thirty to two. In the most recent year, no murders at all occurred in the city of Aurora.[44] In this case, the result was not just an improvement in the "numbers"—it literally saved lives.

One final story.

The 4 Disciplines Takes Flight With the U.S. Navy

In an effort to both significantly increase production of rebuilt F/A-18 Strike Fighter aircraft while simultaneously reducing costs, the U.S. Navy's Fleet Readiness Center Southeast (FRC SE) faced high customer demands due to the Global War on Terror, heavy top-line budget pressures, and fierce competition from other government and commercial depots. FRC leaders partnered with FranklinCovey to focus on delivering 16 F/A-18 aircraft to the Navy in FY 2007 (a year-over-year increase of 77 percent) and reduce costs by $1 million per aircraft. These were goals the depot had never achieved. In addition to driving these two key metrics, they looked to create a performance culture that rewarded both teams and individuals through increased accountability.

Efforts began with assessing the FRC's current ability to focus on and execute key organizational priorities. The process allowed the voices of 242 production and support

44. Kristen Zambo, Andre Salles, "Dramatically Improving the Quality of Life in Aurora, Illinois," *The Beacon News*, Feb. 15, 2007. http://www.highbeam.com/doc/1N1-118383ABA5340088.html

personnel to be heard by senior leaders. Their collective voices showed a lack of clarity on production-line priorities and an unclear path for creating significant improvements. Armed with this information, senior leaders began a process of clarifying the performance gaps, establishing the measures of success, and determining the Wildly Important Goals (WIGs) and initial lead measures. From there, the leaders knew they should not merely announce the goals; rather, they needed to engage employees in creating a shared agreement. These leaders recognized that without involvement, there truly is no commitment.

Senior leaders, managers, front-line artisans, and production-support personnel worked together over a monthlong period to craft the Wildly Important Goals in a way that cascaded to all levels of the organization. To many, the process was difficult, counterintuitive, and revolutionary. Imagine that each team leader nominated draft WIGs and allowed the front line to comment on their worthiness and their individual buy-in to the WIGs. In a hierarchical organization that stressed—even rewarded—command and control, leaders began to ask their people, "How good are our processes?" In the subsequent months, everyone realized that the execution process is biased toward the voice of the front line because that is where F/A-18s get built. It encourages everyone, regardless of role, to lead.

Due to the increased (and consistent) accountability around specific performance goals, leaders actually increased trust with the employees. Likewise, employees enjoyed their increased decision making in figuring out how to best accomplish the mission.

On 17 September 2007, the F/A-18 line, using its pulsed single piece flow line, successfully met its annual production schedule with 16 consecutive pulses and 16 aircraft produced to promised delivery dates; **a 77 percent YTD production-delivery improvement**. Prior to this, the line had never even **once** pulsed on time. Cost savings have been substantial, **reducing 9,834 direct man-hours per aircraft. At $105 per labor hour, that constitutes a savings of $1.032M per aircraft.** The line now has a deliberate process to continue to improve both schedule and costs, allowing managers and employees the ability to optimize team performance.

We have seen results like these in a wide range of environments. Whether processing staff actions, policing city streets, developing complex policies, or identifying and reducing technology risks, leaders and teams have successfully implemented *The 4 Disciplines of Execution* through government organizations. Why? Because the process isn't about one type of work or one specific goal, it's about human behavior. We didn't develop this process with employee engagement in mind. We were focused on execution. Happily, both came as a result. Deep down, we all want to win. *The 4 Disciplines* helps people to go from playing not to lose to truly playing to win. That's what transformation looks like.

CHAPTER 7

PRACTICE 3: UNLEASH PRODUCTIVITY

DISCOVERING THE UNTAPPED POTENTIAL OF EVERY TEAM MEMBER

-

"If you want to build a ship, don't herd people together to collect wood and don't assign them tasks and work, but rather teach them to long for the endless immensity of the sea."

–Antoine de St. Exupéry

-

The great Archimedes (287–212 BCE), one of the world's finest mathematicians, was a man before his time. Not only did he invent integral calculus and figure the approximate value of π (pi), he is also said to be the father of the Machine Age by discovering and putting to use the properties of levers and pulleys.

In a letter to his friend, King Hiero II of Syracuse, Archimedes said, "Give me a place to stand and I will move the world." The king took him up on this claim and had the largest merchant ship of the age, the *Alexandria*, deliberately beached by a team of thousands of slaves and horses and fully loaded with cargo. For days they struggled and strained to ground the giant vessel. Then the king challenged Archimedes to move the ship back into the water by himself.

The story goes that Archimedes attached to the ship a complex machine made of levers and pulleys and, sitting at some distance from the port, gently pulled a rope through the machine. To the amazement of the king, the ship moved in a straight line back into the water. By applying the principle of leverage, Archimedes alone did the work of thousands of men.

Given enough support, any human being has virtually limitless power. Each person in your organization is unique and has an irreplaceable set of gifts, talents, skills, and passions that cannot be found anywhere else. Too many leaders have the pernicious paradigm that people are interchangeable, that one worker equals another, that they can easily replace one person with another person. They see a person as an asset, like a computer or a tractor or a robot, easily traded on the market.

Given enough support, any human being has virtually limitless power.

It's common in government to speak of people as assets, and leaders often toss out the dull cliché that "our people are our most important assets." But people are not assets. An asset is something you *own*—a human being cannot be owned, bought, sold, traded, swapped, exchanged, or returned like a machine.

Too many leaders treat people like machines. You can buy a car, fuel it, wash it occasionally, and take it in once a year for scheduled maintenance and keep it running without much thought. If something goes wrong, you can get it fixed or trade it in for a new one. Often leaders do the same with people: they buy a worker, pay her, and bring her in once a year for a performance review to make sure she is "doing what it takes" to achieve the organization's productivity goals. If something goes wrong, they get her "fixed" (send her over to HR), trade her in for a new one, or shift her someplace else in the organization, making her "someone else's problem." The leader shakes his head, wondering why that employee is not as excited or motivated as he to give a little "extra effort."

The old industrial paradigm that an employee is an interchangeable cog in the machine is the most important reason why people are disengaged in the workplace, refusing to give the "extra effort." That's why the most important job to be done now is to replace that paradigm with a new paradigm: *Every person is uniquely powerful.* Your job as a leader is to unleash that power.

For years now, the mantra of government leaders throughout the world has been "do more with less." Cut costs, leverage assets, maximize efficiencies—and it's a good paradigm, as everyone knows. The problem is, it isn't sufficient anymore. Some leaders even use that mantra to abuse people, loading more and more work on them without giving them the right kind of support. More often, leaders simply don't understand the principle of leverage. Remember Archimedes: One person has virtually limitless power, given the right mindset, the right tools, and the right place to stand.

The job used to be...	The job you must do now...
Do more with less.	Unleash people to choose to do infinitely more than you imagined they could.

The new mantra is this: "Unleash people and they will choose to do infinitely more than you ever imagined they could."

In the Industrial Age, we leashed people to the ship and instructed them to drag it; it was hard work, but they did it. Now, if you're mentally still stuck with that mindset, you have fewer people leashed to the ship and you're piling on cargo (it's called "more with less"); so they're getting burned out instead of fired up, exhausted instead of energized. This is not the way to engage them.

The "more with less" trend was going on long before the financial crisis of the twenty-first century, which made things substantially worse. Many government agencies saw budget cuts, staff reductions, and greater resources limitations. Those left behind have been taking on more and more excessive workloads, putting real strain on family life and social relationships.

Now a third of Americans are experiencing chronic work stress.[45] According to the *Journal of the American Medical Association,* only 13 percent of Americans in middle age are healthier than their parents were at the same age: the doctors say chronic stress is the number-one reason.[46] And it's not just the older workers who suffer; a vast number of professionals are burning out in their thirties; it's particularly tough for

45. Ron Breazeale, "In the Face of Adversity," *Psychology Today*, Apr. 1, 2013. http://www.psychologytoday.com/blog/in-the-face-adversity/201304/your-job

46. Donna Jackson Na.k.a.zawa, "The American Stress-Illness Crisis," *Psychology Today*, May 13, 2013. http://www.psychologytoday.com/blog/the-last-best-cure/201305/the-american-stress-illness-crisis

younger women who have to deal with the "double shift" of work and motherhood.[47]

When the broader economy suffers, government workers often see an uptick in workload, stress, and burnout. In late 2009, the world economy was suffering the challenges of the recession. As a result, countless government workers were dealing with more work and fewer resources. The public-sector innovation publication *eRepublic* reported that when the Nevada unemployment rate hit 13.2 percent, "the caseload for that state's Temporary Assistance for Needy Families (TANF) program has grown 30%; the Medicaid caseload, 20%; and the food-stamp caseload, 45%. When eligibility workers in larger district offices in Las Vegas and Reno open the doors in the morning, there are already 100 to 125 people standing in line. Meanwhile, all government workers—including Medicaid and TANF caseworkers—now are required to take off one day a month. The result: Employees have seen their portfolios expand like a balloon that's about to pop, and the clients they see are frustrated and angry about the long waits they have to endure."[48]

Burnout is a worldwide problem. In Britain, work-related mental health conditions such as stress, depression, and

47. Larissa Faw, "Why Some Women Are Burning Out at Work by 30," *Forbes*, Nov. 22, 2011. http://www.nbcnews.com/id/45357267/ns/business-forbes_com/t/why-some-women-are-burning-out-work/?fb_ref=.TsvEvx98ch4.like&fb_source=home_multiline#.Ugbz8pKsim7

48. "Government and the Stress Mess" *eRepublic*, December 2009.

anxiety cost UK employers about £28.3 billion a year.[49] In India's fast-growing tech sector, "exhaustion and cynicism have increased"[50] and "stress is becoming a huge deterrent to productivity."[51] In Japan, 10,000 working people die each year from *karoshi,* the Japanese term for "death from overwork."[52]

In Japan, 10,000 working people die each year from karoshi, the Japanese term for "death from overwork."

There comes a point where fewer workers trying to do too much simply can't drag the ship any farther—and we seem to be coming to that point. McKinsey & Company has concluded that global productivity is stalling precisely because of an underdeveloped, unleveraged workforce: "To eke out even modest GDP increases, OECD nations must achieve nothing short of Herculean gains in productivity.

49. "Are You Suffering From Job Burnout"? *CareerBuilder UK*, Aug. 26, 2011. http://www.careerbuilder.co.uk/article/cb-361-workplace-issues-are-you-suffering-from-job-burnout/

50. Panjak Singh, "Health Consequences and Buffers of Burnout Among Indian Software Developers," *Psychological Studies*, Nov. 2, 2012. http://link.springer.com/article/10.1007%2Fs12646-012-0171-9#page-2

51. Yasmin Taj, "India Inc. in Need of an Anti-Stress Pill," *Ezenus*, Apr. 7, 2013. http://www.ezenus.com/index.php/home?n=39

52. Jane Weaver, "Job Stress, Burnout on the Rise," *NBC News*, Sept. 1, 2003. http://www.nbcnews.com/id/3072410/ns/business-us_business/t/job-stress-burnout-rise/#.Ugb7lpKsim4

In the 1970s, the United States could rely on a growing labor force to generate 80 cents of every $1 gain in GDP. During the coming decade, that ratio will invert: labor-force gains will contribute less than 30 cents to each additional dollar of economic growth.... The challenge is even greater in Western Europe, where no growth in the workforce is expected.... And in Japan, the hurdle is higher still."[53]

Unleashing the Power of People

That's why your accomplishing your organization's mission today, tomorrow, and into the future will be a function of your ability to unleash the latent productivity of people.

Scientists tell us there is enough nuclear energy in a few buckets of seawater to power the entire world for a day—if it could be unleashed. Likewise, there's enough talent, intelligence, capability, and creativity in each of the people in your organization to astound you—if it could be unleashed. Dr. Stephen Covey said, "Imagine the personal and organizational cost of failing to fully engage the passion, talent, and intelligence of the workforce. It is far greater than you can possibly imagine."

In the Industrial Age, money was the key motivator. Many government leaders claim that when their people exhibit a

---

53. "The Productivity Imperative," *McKinsey & Company*, June 2010. http://www.mckinsey.com/global-themes/employment-and-growth/the-productivity-imperative

low level of engagement, it is because the leader lacks the financial means to incentivize them. Perhaps there is some truth to this argument, but in many cases, the problem runs deeper than money. The reality is that financial incentives fall short of engaging people: Salary is a "hygiene factor"—it's expected. So, what does motivate them? A monumental Towers-Perrin study shows that knowing their contribution is valued means far more to workers than their salary does. No other motivational factor—money, opportunity, trust, or communication—counts as much as "appreciation."[54] To know that your contribution is meaningful matters more than anything else.

Knowing their contribution is valued means far more to workers than their salary does.

"The least of things with meaning is worth more in life than the greatest of things without it," said Carl Jung. Almost every worker feels this way, as scholars recently found when surveying people across generations. It doesn't much matter how old we are or the kind of work we do: "We all want the same basic things out of work," concludes Wharton Professor Adam Grant. "Whether we're Boomers,

---

54. Towers-Perrin, *Turbocharging Employee Engagement*, 2010. http://www.towersperrin.com/tp/getwebcachedoc?country=gbr&webc=GBR/2009/200909/White_Paper_Turbocharging_Employee_Engagement_Sept_09_Part_2.pdf

Gen Xers, or Millennials, we're searching for *interesting, meaningful jobs* that challenge and stretch us."[55]

Meaning is the key to engaging people. It's more important than money. It's even more important than happiness. In her research, psychologist Dr. Barbara Fredrickson found that "even at the molecular level, our physical and psychological well-being is more dependent on meaning than on happiness." Too much "feel-good living" seems to increase inflammation, higher stress levels, and a weaker immune system, whereas "meaningful living" is associated with better immune responses and capacity to handle adversity.[56] Meaning is good for you. It's also good for the organization you work for—the more people find their work meaningless, the worse it is for the organization.

Some will say, "It's my job to pay them. It's their job to find meaning in what they do." They have the old organizational mindset described by Daniel Pink: "Humans by their nature seek purpose—to make a contribution and to be part of a cause greater and more enduring than themselves. But traditional bureaucracies have long considered purpose

---

55. Adam Grant, "What Millennials Really Want Out of Work," *Huffington Post Blog*, Aug. 2, 2013. http://www.huffingtonpost.com/adam-grant/millennial-generation-jobs_b_3696622.html. Italics added.

56. Barbara Fredrickson, *Positivity: Top-notch Research Reveals the 3 to 1 Ratio That Will Change Your Life* , Harmony, 2009.

ornamental—a perfectly nice accessory, so long as it didn't get in the way of the important things."[57]

The other vitally important component to unleashing a person's power is a sense of accomplishment. One can know his purpose and be passionate about it, but in today's world of do more with less, where government employees are more accessible (thanks to technology), buffed by demands, crises, matrixed teams, and more, he may be left wondering why, at the end of each day, he was so busy but felt so unaccomplished. Think about your organization: have you developed a culture of "busy"? Is your culture one where the award goes to the person who stayed latest at night versus the one who executed perfectly on a key project or goal and still left at a reasonable hour? Have you created a culture of "reward for rescue at the eleventh hour," instead of reward for a great root-cause analysis that removed a chronic issue and made a difference for those you serve? Have you provided the processes and methods that allow high-impact projects to get completed on time and with high quality, reducing both redundancy and rework? Have you equipped your people with the communication skills to powerfully and precisely inform and persuade others to action to reduce the disease of unproductive meetings?

---

57. Daniel Pink, *Drive: The Surprising Truth About What Motivates Us*, Riverhead Books, 2011, 223.

Think about your organization: have you developed a culture of "busy"?

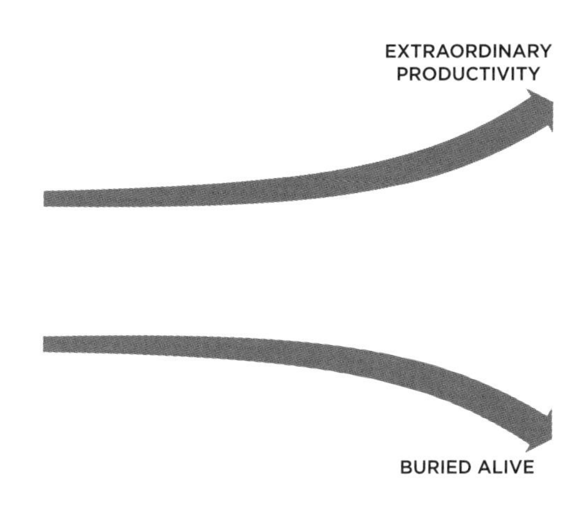

Nobody wants to be buried under a load of meaningless assignments or just busywork pushing through to the voluminous number of deadlines to hit. If the work isn't engaging people and they are not equipped with the tools to execute with excellence, you need to back up and think seriously about how you expect your people to execute on their best efforts in the Knowledge Worker Age. Your peoples' greatest assets are their brains, no longer just the hands and backs that were required of the Industrial Age. We are well out of the Industrial Age, and it's time more government leaders come to terms with this. As Peter Drucker said, "The most important, and indeed the truly unique, contribution of management in the twentieth century was the fifty-fold increase in the productivity of the manual worker. The most important contribution management needs to make in the twenty-first century is similarly to increase the productivity of knowledge work and the knowledge worker…." So, what are the root problems for the knowledge workers of the twenty-first century?

Twenty-First-Century Productivity Barriers

FranklinCovey has been the leader in time management for many years. We've trained more than 25 million people and enabled that learning with our famous Franklin Planner tools. We've helped people manage "time." Today's productivity problems go far deeper than just managing units of time. The knowledge-worker world has a few specific challenges that allow time to just "go by," and can leave us feeling unaccomplished and weary at the end of a day.

Productivity Problem 1

We are making more decisions than ever before. Think about it. Every email, demand, request, phone call, and/or idea is a decision your brain is required to make. During the Industrial Age, workers on an assembly line put one part on one machine a hundred times a day. They had few choices and fewer decisions to make. Decisions they did have to make were simple and of low value. Their tools had one straightforward use.

As knowledge workers, we no longer stand in an assembly line doing repetitive tasks. We have comparatively unlimited decisions coming at us about what to work on, when and how. (For example: Do I answer this email? accept this meeting invitation? work on this project or that one?) You do your best handling decisions as they come in, but the decisions you are required to make are complex and have high value. For example, a case worker's decisions on how to use her time can mean a life is saved or lost. One might be constantly busy but still ask the at the end of the day, "What the heck did I get done?"

One might be constantly busy but still ask the at the end of the day, "What the heck did I get done?"

One of our government clients told us that her leadership team was overrun with emails, meetings to attend, fires to put out, and other demands. They were just too, too busy. When asked what the most important activities were to moving the organization forward, she explained that spending time as a leadership team discussing the big challenges facing the organization and coming together on plans to overcome them was key to long-term agency success. Every leader on her team knew that, but all them were so "busy," the important discussions were not being chosen as the high-priority activities. Guess what? The addiction to "busyness" plagued every level of this complex agency.

Productivity Problem 2

At the same time, our attention is under unprecedented attack. The dings, pings, beeps, and buzzes each represent a demand and seem to come at us from everywhere. Thanks to technology, the information explosion is huge. But it is almost incomprehensible how huge. By the end of the twentieth century, the entire sum of information produced since the dawn of civilization was about 12 exabytes. We now produce this much information in about four days! And that does not include our personal information. We are all in serious danger of drowning in emails, texts, and tweets! The fact that our brain loves the novelty of those dings and pings doesn't help, and creates an addiction to technology. Thus the paradox: technology makes our life easier, more effective, and efficient, but it also distracts us and overburdens us because the unstoppable flow of information is out of control.

Productivity Problem 3

Problems 1 and 2 are wearing us out. We suffer from a personal energy crisis. We no longer work a standard eight-hour day. Our minds are constantly churning trying to make high-value decisions, virtually twenty-four hours a day. Our mode of life today—constant stress, poor diet, and lack of exercise and sleep—leads to what scientists call "exhaustion syndrome." The rest of us call it burnout. We continually "push through" each day, postponing the renewal time our body and brain need. The mantra is "work like crazy and then crash." And as we mentioned earlier, we get rewarded for the ordinary mindset; it becomes a badge of honor to brag, "Our team was up till midnight." Do your employees receive emails and texts from you at 10 p.m? Chances are, they are stressed, not knowing whether they should be answering those or not. Are they supposed to "work" at that hour? Do they know what you expect?

The mantra is "work like crazy and then crash."

Some leaders will shrug these problems off, saying, "This is just the world we have to live in. Deal with it." Highly effective leaders will realize the costs of this and take action.

In an ongoing FranklinCovey survey of more than 350,000 people at all levels from around the world, respondents self-reported that they felt they were wasting 40 percent of their time.[58] That's almost half their time!

These vast losses don't blatantly show up as expenses on the P&L or as a liability on the balance sheet. Yet, they are global and they are pervasive. And most important? Wasting half your time is completely disengaging.

The more these three problems are managed, the more extraordinary you and your teams will be. If we ignore the fact that it is no longer just about "time management," your workforce will continue to not feel accomplished, not feel like they serve a purpose, and disengage.

58. Kory Kogan, et al, *The 5 Choices: The Path to Extraordinary Productivity*, New York: Simon & Schuster, 2015, 12.

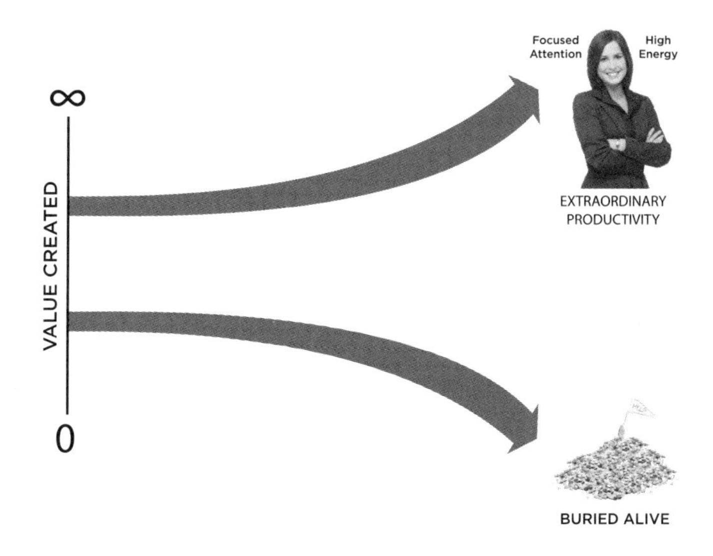

But imagine if they did feel accomplished, did enjoy coming to work, and knew every day they were making a great contribution? What would it mean if your teams measurably reported they felt they were working on important things 80 or 90 percent of the time instead of 60 percent? What would it mean to their level of engagement if most of their time was productive? And what would that focus mean to your ability to accomplish your team's mission?

So how do we capture what people can produce when they "put their mind and heart" into it? By equipping them with twenty-first-century mindsets, skillsets, and toolsets that assist them in feeling highly accomplished every day.

High productivity and team engagement start with you. Are you modeling the right productivity behaviors? Are you intentionally sorting through all the incoming stuff, making the highest-value decisions every day? Are you conscious of how many decisions—with varying levels of urgency—you ask your people to make every day that may cause overload? Do you realize your people tend to assume you need everything right now?

Are you conscious of how you use your technology, making sure you rule your technology versus letting it rule you? The greatest way to disengage employees is to peek at your smartphone when they come to you asking you for help or just during a casual conversation. Your brain can only do one thing well at a time; if it is trying to process smartphone information, there is no way you can hear or connect with the person trying to get your attention. And if that is your behavior, you have trained your team to do the same.

Are you known as the "inhuman" that works practically twenty-four hours a day with no breaks? Is this a badge of honor? Studies show that pausing, resting, and sleeping increase productivity by 35 percent. Modeling this behavior is critical. Once your people see you mastering the art of making the highest-value decisions, staying focused on *humans* instead of just *technology*, and taking care of your (and their) mental and physical energy, the faster everyone will expand their contribution.

We were presenting once on the topic of productivity to a group of government employees in central Florida. At one point, we asked everyone to write down 10 to 15 reoccurring activities they perform each week. We then asked them to label each item as important or unimportant, and urgent or not urgent. When they finished the task, we invited them to pair up and discuss what they wrote.

We remember listening in on a discussion between two women at the front table. The first woman, a new employee to the organization, said that the weekly staff meetings were both important and urgent. The words barely emerged before the second woman, a seasoned co-worker, interrupted with a curt, "Yes, they are urgent because our boss tells us to drop everything and get in the meeting room, but if you go to enough of our staff meetings, you will learn that we learn nothing new. They are a colossal waste of time." The first employee's face revealed the look of someone's disengagement level going to zero."

Later in the day, we had a chance to talk to their supervisor. We didn't say, "Let me tell you what your employees are saying about you." We simply asked the boss how things were going, and allowed the conversation to steer itself to the exercise. The supervisor conveyed that the weekly staff meetings were important but not urgent. A brief discussion followed, in which the boss admitted he often shifted the time of the meetings because his schedule was frantic. Furthermore, he revealed that nearly every meeting covered the same issues and little was truly learned from the conversation. The meetings had become more obligatory than useful. Essentially, the boss confirmed what the seasoned employee had stated.

It was like a light went on in his head. The supervisor realized he wasn't treating the meetings as important, and that he was creating an unnecessary level of stress on his staff. He vowed in that moment to change the way he dealt with his staff meetings."

Several weeks later, we received an unsolicited email from the seasoned employee. She explained that at the first staff meeting following the workshop, her supervisor started the session by stating he believed that the staff meetings were ineffective and he owned making them that way. She said you could've heard a pin drop. The supervisor further explained he was concerned that he and others on the team had become addicted to busyness.

From that moment, things changed. The team began speaking a common language of *importance*. They challenged long-existing processes, started to use technology more effectively, and began supporting one another's efforts to take better care of themselves. We saw disengagement in the eyes of the new employee during the workshop. But we saw engagement reappear in the words that jumped from the screen as the experienced employee shared how things had dramatically changed." Does this work?

Stephanie, aged twenty-four, and a new elementary school teacher, shared an insight she gained about her contribution in life: "As a new teacher, I had a parent tell me that her son was a better person for having known me. Those words had a significant impact on me. I realized that I don't have to be well known to make a difference. A contribution of this sort cannot be measured in the way the world measures success, but the effects are never-ending. I want to leave that legacy."

You engage individuals by helping them discover the contribution they want to make in their roles. We each have one or more roles to play in the organization's success. Some people sell, some design products, some do marketing, some process or analyze data and financials. Some are on matrixed teams, some are mentors or coaches. We each have at least one job, one role to do, and in today's world, many have more. But we should not be our job descriptions, whether at work or even at home. It is not so much what we do but the reason behind what we do that motivates us. We create the vision of success for our roles.

You engage individuals by helping them discover the contribution they want to make in their roles.

What roles do you play? What is your vision of success in your roles? When you determine this, you will rediscover passion and purpose. So will your people. When they discover and write down the purpose in their role (what they want to be known for in their role), they are identifying the burning contribution they would love to make.

You get a clear sense of who these people are, what their gifts are, and what their philosophies about their work are. People are full of passion and realism. And you need to model effective behaviors and then help identify and unleash the power of volunteered productivity from your team.

Take a minute to think about your leadership role. Write a statement that describes the contribution you want to make. Don't just describe what you do now. Write down what you *want* to do in your leadership role. In this way, you'll tap into your own passion, discovering what really motivates you and how you can create a better world around you.

W.H. Murray, organizer of the 1951 Scottish Himalayan expedition, wrote: "Until one is committed, there is hesitancy, the chance to draw back, always ineffectiveness concerning all acts of initiative and creation. There is one elementary truth, the ignorance of which kills countless ideas and splendid plans; that the moment one definitely commits oneself, then Providence moves too.

"All sorts of things occur to help one that would never otherwise have occurred. A whole stream of events issues from the decision raising in one's favor all manner of unforeseen events, meetings, and material assistance which no one could have dreamed would have come their way."

It is amazing what happens when you pause from the "busyness" for a moment, reach inside, and find your purpose and make a commitment to your role statement. When your purpose is combined with determined action, you create a sense of momentum that is hard to stop. This is what it means to live by design rather than by default. When people know the vision for success in their roles, it accelerates high-value decision management and focused attention

You can help others discover their contribution by having this conversation with them:

> "Imagine meeting yourself when you leave your current role, whether it's weeks, months, or years from now. Who are you? What contributions have you made? How do you know? Have you made a real difference to the

organization? to the people we serve? How would you define and measure that difference?

"Have you given the best that's in you? Have you brought your best talents, gifts, and creativity to the role? In what ways? Have you felt yourself stretching, growing, learning? How have you grown? What is the most important thing you've learned?"

As people contemplate these questions, they go deep into themselves. They tap into what invigorates them and what is the root of their passion. Simply put, they engage. If you challenge your people in this way, you will be the rarest of leaders—the one who knows how to release the tremendous inner power of your people.

And you *will* be rare. According to McKinsey & Company, "Despite the dramatic changes in the way people work, the organizations in which they carry out that work have changed much less than might be expected.... Today's [large organizations] do very little to enhance the productivity of their professionals."[59] In other words, twenty-first-century organizations are not fit for twenty-first-century workers.

59. "The New Organisation," Special Report, *The Economist*, Jan. 19, 2006, 3.

> **"Today's [large organizations] do very little to enhance the productivity of their professionals."**
> **—McKinsey & Company**

Tapping Untold Energies

Be the rare leader who turns this situation around. Contemplate the energy, vitality, and optimism of people who are deeply engaged, particularly in this era when our technology leaves us breathless. We are at the edge of the greatest of times. Mayor Gavin Newsom of San Francisco has this insight: "The reality is, people will build cool things for the sake of building cool things. They will expend countless hours and untold energy for the sake of creating something useful or even just fun. There's an excitement out there, a hunger to try new things, to explore the limits of what all these new technologies can do."[60]

But we can still see you shaking your head. "There's so much apathy out there. People have been knocked around and messed with and worked to the bone. I don't know if they would have the energy to 'engage' even if they wanted

60. Gavin Newsom, *Citizenville: How to Take the Town Square Digital and Reinvent Government*, Penguin Books, 2014, 11.

to. They've been dragging the ship through the mud for so long that their souls are burned out."

"Apathy doesn't actually exist," says Canadian startup genius Dave Meslin. "People do care, but we live in a world that actively discourages engagement by constantly putting obstacles in our way.

"We're missing the most important characteristic of leadership, which is that it comes from within, it means following your own dreams *uninvited*, and then working with others to make your dreams come true. Companies are so uninspiring and uncreative, feeding cynicism at the expense of bold and creative ideas. Of course, people are apathetic. It's like running into a brick wall."[61] You don't have to work in a startup to see this challenge. Look around your office, talk to your co-workers, and see what you learn.

Karen and Bob Hahne were in their forties, with a house full of young children, when they received a call at home one evening. Karen happened to answer the phone. It was social services. The Hahnes had adopted three children years before, so it wasn't entirely unusual to receive a call from social services. The caller told her they had just learned of a baby boy who needed a home and asked if Karen would be interested in adopting another child. "This child was

---

61. Dave Meslin, "The Antidote to Apathy," *TED.com*, Apr 2011.

born with Down syndrome. He will have many special challenges and will require unique care."

So they started a new adventure with their new son, Reed. Something about him engaged their souls and a fierce outpouring of energy.

As anticipated, Reed presented many challenges. The professionals told them to "love him, but don't expect too much." Others advised to keep Reed out of the school system. He would be figuratively crucified, they were told. Another concerned individual asked them, "How can you do this to your other children?" Their response, "How can we not give them this wonderful opportunity to learn and grow?"

Over the next few years, the Hahnes worked with Reed. As expected, his development was delayed, but progress began. Gradually, Reed responded to their care. They exposed him to fine music, the theatre, and other culturally rich and stimulating experiences. Reed learned to talk, exuding enthusiasm for life. The Hahnes continued to explore every possibility for helping Reed grow in capability. They pursued government and community initiatives, only to learn there were few options. But they decided not to sit and fret about it. Learning of other parents of Downs children who also struggled for resources and support, they started a small group called "Up With Downs Early

Preschool," which met a couple of days a week in a local high school. There both children and parents could learn and help each other.

Word began to spread. More and more parents came seeking education and support. Two mothers wrote a grant proposal and, much to their surprise, got it. The program, known as "Kids on the Move," grew beyond those facilities, and it became clear they needed their own building. With little funding and escalating demand, the Hahnes and other parents persevered. They begged for money, got government grants, and enlisted the help of a generous community. Today Kids on the Move is a substantial school for children from birth to age three, and the program's influence extends well beyond the school deep into homes and communities. The program currently serves more than 1,500 families each year, and employees 80 people.

And Reed? This young man, whom "experts" considered a hopeless case, has grown into a wonderful contributor to society. Not only did he learn to talk, he learned to excel. He attended a unique high school where he had many friends. For their school "Preference" dance, Reed was voted one of the school's "most preferred," and he successfully served on student council his senior year. He went to college and got excellent grades. He is a regular speaker at youth events. He has won awards for advocacy and addressed many national groups. Not bad for a young man who wasn't expected to accomplish anything.

Once ignited, Karen and Bob Hahnes' passion became an amazing productive force. They faced hardship, discouragement, and the occasional dead end; but their perseverance has benefited thousands of lives and brought hope to many families with nowhere else to turn.

The secret to productivity is to ignite the passions of your team.

The first step in unleashing people is to engage the passion they innately possess and the legacy they want to leave. You don't have to invite them to have dreams—they already have them. The secret to quantum leaps in productivity is to find that leverage point of meaning that gives life to the human soul.

The secret to productivity is to ignite the passions of your team.

Unleashing Productivity: Instructions for Downloading

Here are five choices you can make to master making the highest highest-value decisions, stay focused, and have the energy to unleash your own productivity and the productivity of others:

Step	Actions
1. Act on the Important, Don't React to the Urgent	Make a list of all the things you do during a typical work week. All of them. Don't forget email inboxes, papers that need attention, social-media updates, phone calls to return, people to get back to.

Draw four boxes that look like this. Label the boxes as indicated.

1. Urgent and Important	**2. Important, Not Urgent**
3. Urgent, Not Important	**4. Not Urgent, Not Important**

Drop each action item from your list into one of the four boxes as indicated. Then follow these recommendations:

Box	Action Items	Reccommendation
1	Important and urgent things, like putting out fires, taking care of emergencies, meeting close deadlines, etc.	Do them and then analyze how to prevent them in the future. If you are honest, you will see that many of the things in Box 1 could have been avoided if you had prepared for them.
2	Important but not urgent things, like planning your time, working on long-term goals, continuous improvement, preventing future crises, reading, and learning.	Focus your best time and energies here. If you do, you will have plenty of time for the things that really matter.
3	Unimportant things that are urgent, like some requests from other people, meetings you've been invited to but don't really need to attend, etc.	Say no when possible to these things. A lot of what people ask you to do might not contribute at all to your top goals and personal priorities—and might even be better handled by someone else.
4	Unimportant things that are not urgent, excessive behavior.	Hold yourself accountable to these things. Don't let relaxation or break time turn into excess, taking away from more important outcomes.

When you identified the activities in the four boxes, did you limit your responses to "work activities" only? Go back and list all your other activities in your personal and family life as well.

Invite your team to go through this exercise. Ask: "What are we doing in Boxes 3 and 4 that we shouldn't be doing at all? What are the things in Box 1 that we wouldn't have to do if we did better preparation work? What are the things in Box 2 that we should focus on?"

Step	Actions
2. Go for Extraordinary, Don't Settle for Ordinary	As a leader, your task is to unleash the extraordinary potential of people, but first you need to find out what their potential is. You can discover it by having this conversation: "Imagine meeting yourself when you leave your current role, whether it's weeks, months, or years from now... • Who are you? How have you changed? • What contributions have you made? How do you know? Have you made a real difference to the organization? to our clients? How would you define and measure that difference? • Have you given the best that's in you? Have you brought your best talents, gifts, and creativity to the role? In what ways? • Have you felt yourself stretching, growing, and learning? How have you grown? What is the most important thing you've learned?

Carry out this experiment for yourself before trying it on others:

- **Identify the few most important roles you play and write them down.** List your work roles and your "outside of work" roles.

- **Write a contribution statement that describes the extraordinary contribution you want to make in each role.** Take your time. Don't just describe what you do now, write down what you *want* to do in your current role. In this way, you'll tap into your own passion, discovering what really motivates you and how you can create a better world around you and feel accomplished at the end of every day.

Role	Contribution Statement

Do this exercise with team members. Invite people to write down the answers to these questions on their own and then share them with you.

Step	Actions
3. Schedule Your Priorities, Don't Prioritize Your Schedule	Each week look closely at your calendar. Then use the "box exercise" from step 1 to plan the week. Check off each of the following actions:
	Look at your role statements. Which one or two key things can you do this week that will have the most impact on your vision of success? These are your Box 2 actions. Schedule them. List all other action items and drop them into the boxes. Leave Box 1 items in your calendar, but ask yourself how you could avoid them in the future. Plan to do so. Delete or delegate Box 3 items. They are not important. Delete Box 4 items. They are not important. Make sure you do NOT delete some relaxation, break, or leisure time. This is most likely a Box 2 item.

The biggest threat to your productivity is the very technology designed to accelerate it—your smartphone, your laptop, or your tablet. As is typical, you might say hello to your tablet first thing in the morning. You check your mail, you're reading it during breakfast, then you're playing games, surfing, checking out social media, doing research all day. You're on your smartphone too, constantly texting, ringing people up, texting again, and texting some more. At night, the last thing you see as you fall asleep is the glow of a screen.

The technology is amazingly useful, but it also distracts us and, even worse, can rule our lives.

Step	Actions
4. Rule Your Technology, Don't Let It Rule You	Schedule times to check your device to avoid the "constant glance." Stay away from your devices when engaged with people.
	Invite your team to think through their philosophy about technology. How can you use it better? Are you caught in a web of electronic distractions? How can you eliminate them?

You and your team have a big mission that involves intensive work, so you can't afford to burn out. Keep the fire burning, but in a balanced way. Brain scientists agree that proper exercise, diet, sleep, relaxation, and human connection recharge and even rejuvenate the brain.

Fuel Your Fire, Don't Burn Out	Schedule times to "refuel" yourself. One of your key roles is "self."
	Invite your team to make personal plans to take care of these priorities.

CHAPTER 8

PRACTICE 4: INSPIRE TRUST

WHY CHARACTER AND COMPETENCE MATTER AND WHAT TO DO ABOUT IT

-

"Trust is the most overlooked, misunderstood, underutilized asset an organization can access."
–Stephen M. R. Covey

-

In his classic book *The Speed of Trust*, our friend and colleague Stephen M. R. Covey explained that the first imperative of a leader—at work or at home—is to inspire trust. It's to bring out the best in people by entrusting them with meaningful stewardships and create an environment in which high-trust interaction inspires engagement, creativity, and possibility.

Given this, maybe no other job of a highly effective leader is more pressing than to inspire trust in those he or she is leading. Your job is to model trustworthiness and help your team members become high-trust individuals.

Investing time in the development of trust among your team is a smart investment and is critical to creating long-term, sustainable mission success.

The opposite can have dire consequences. Loss of trust is arguably the main reason we have been mired in a dreary economy. The repeated financial shocks of the twenty-first century have produced steep declines in public trust in bedrock institutions like big business, banking, and government. Many have lost faith in the foundations of society.

Let's consider the impact of low trust in businesses. Only 10 percent of workers trust their bosses to do the right thing, and only 14 percent believe their company's leaders are ethical and honest.[62] Less than a fifth of the general public trusts business leaders to be ethical and honest.[63] Only 16 percent of Americans trust large corporations.[64] And 82 percent of workers believe that their senior leaders help themselves at the organization's expense. They look at their leaders and see too much self-interest, short-term focus, and ego-driven decision making.

---

62. Jeanette Mulvey, "American Workers Don't Trust Their Bosses," *BusinessNewsDaily*, Jul. 12, 2011. http://www.businessnewsdaily.com/1195-employees-dont-trust-bosses.html

63. Geoffrey James, "Warning: Customers Don't Trust Leaders," *Inc.*, April 19, 2013. http://www.inc.com/geoffrey-james/warning-customers-dont-trust-leaders.html

64. "Anger Over Economy Remains," *Chicago Booth/Kellogg School Financial Trust Index*, May 31, 2013. http://www.financialtrustindex.org/

82% of workers believe that their senior leaders help themselves at the organization's expense.

Oxford University Professor Colin Mayer diagnoses the situation this way: "The loss of trust in the corporation reflects a belief that it exists simply to make money for its owners, its shareholders, and it will do whatever it takes to achieve this. From our point of view as customers, employees, and communities, we are therefore pawns in a game in which we are manipulated for the benefit of others. The repeated recurrence of scandals only serves to reinforce the belief that the corporation is inherently untrustworthy."[65]

If you think the general low trust in for-profit organizations is sobering, consider how citizens see government. For over fifty years, the Organisation for Economic Cooperation and Development (OECD) has "helped forge global standards, international conventions, agreements, and recommendations in areas such as governance and the fight against bribery and corruption, corporate responsibility, development, international investment, taxes, and the environment."[66] The organization consists of thirty-four-member countries

65. Colin Mayer, Firm Commitment: Why the Corporation Is Failing Us and How to Restore Trust in It, *Oxford Univ. Press*, 2013.

66. 2016 OECD Annual Report. http://www.keepeek.com/Digital-Asset-Management/oecd/economics/secretary-general-s-report-to-ministers-2016_sg_report-2016-en#.WGcPrbGZPfA#page1

including the United States, Australia, the United Kingdom, Mexico, and Japan. In 2014, OECD reported that only 40 percent of citizens trusted their government. "Trust in government is deteriorating in many OECD countries. Lack of trust compromises the willingness of citizens and businesses to respond to public policies and contribute to sustainable economic recovery."[67]

Levels of trust in government differ among countries, but nearly all are reporting unprecedented lows. According to the Pew Research Center, the United States is experiencing historic lows in the public's trust in government. "In 1958, when the American National Election Study first asked the question, 73% [of Americans] said they could trust the government just about always or most of the time.... Only 19% of Americans today say they can trust the government in Washington to do the what is right."[68]

Widespread mistrust acts like a brake on the economy. Everything in the supply chain slows down because transactions have to be regulated, verified, documented, and double-checked. Deals take forever because due diligence is now *intense* diligence. Costs go up at every point. Low levels of trust in government and business conspire to make

67. OECD. "Trust in Government," published in 2014. http://www.oecd.org/gov/trust-in-government.htm

68. Pew Research Center. "Beyond Distrust: How Americans View Their Government," November 23, 2015. http://www.people-press.org/2015/11/23/1-trust-in-government-1958-2015/

everything cost more and take longer. An example: The Sarbanes-Oxley regulations in response to the scandals at Enron and World-Com are unbelievably time-consuming and expensive—one study pegged the costs of implementing just one section of the law at $35 billion!

Trust—A Performance Multiplier

When an individual, a team, or an entire government agency is known for being trusted, the bad news is good news. People, both inside and outside your organization, are hungrier than ever to work with and support people they can trust. At every level of your organization and in every interaction, the "economies of trust" are at work. Consider this: trust always affects two measurable outcomes—speed and cost. When trust goes down, speed goes down and cost goes up. This creates a *Trust Tax*. When trust goes up, speed goes up and cost goes down. This creates a *Trust Dividend*. It's that simple, real, and predictable.

How do you feel about those relationships where trust is high? How effective is your communication with a person you trust? In our experience, it's easy, simple, and fast. Even if we're dealing with a tough issue, it can be resolved with the person quickly. In high-trust relationships, you can misspeak, but you don't feel like you're walking on eggshells, worrying that you'll offend the other person or make a commitment by accident.

Conversely, when trust is low, it seems that no matter what you say, your words are taken wrong or out of context. Communication is nearly impossible, even about the most trivial things.

Shawn tells this story: "During a casual conversation, a colleague once made an offhand promise to me. Over time, things changed and it looked like it would be impossible for him to keep his promise—it wasn't his fault, it was just matter of circumstance. So I was surprised one day when he called to tell me he had finished the work he'd promised to do. Now, this effort came at great personal sacrifice for him, but he'd made a commitment and he was determined to follow through. I had always trusted him, but that day I gained an even deeper and more profound appreciation for his integrity and knew that he could be trusted no matter what. Over the years, he and I have had tough talks about important strategic issues, but our communication has always been quick and easy.

"In contrast, I once had another colleague whose relationship with me was dicey, always clouded by ulterior motives and hidden agendas. Even simple conversations with him were difficult, as nearly every word I said aroused suspicion and offense. It was exhausting, like a slow-motion wrestling match."

Trust is the great accelerator. Where trust is high, everything is faster and less complicated, and where trust is low, everything is slower, costlier, and encumbered with suspicion.

Once we understand the hard-edged, measurable economics of trust, it's like putting on a new pair of glasses. Everywhere we look, we can see quantifiable impact. If we have a low-trust organization, we're paying a tax. While these taxes may not conveniently show up in financial reports as "Trust Taxes," they're still there, disguised as other problems. Once we know where and what to look for, we see low-trust organizational taxes everywhere, including the following: redundancy, bureaucracy, politics, churn, fraud, disengagement, and turnover. Have you ever seen low trust cause people to leave your organization? If so, who typically leaves? More often than not, it's the people you want to stay. Fortunately, just as the taxes created by low trust are significant, the dividends of high trust are also incredibly high.

Trust is the great accelerator. Where trust is high, everything is faster and less complicated, and where trust is low, everything is slower, costlier, and encumbered with suspicion.

When trust is high, the dividend we receive is a *performance multiplier*, elevating and improving every dimension of the organization. Specific dividends include the following: increased alignment, enhanced innovation, improved collaboration, stronger partnering, higher engagement, better execution, and heightened loyalty. When you add up all the dividends of high trust, and you put those on top of the fact that high trust decreases or eliminates all the taxes as well, is there any doubt that there is a significant, direct, measurable and indisputable connection between high trust, high speed, low cost, and increased value? Indeed, trust is the one thing that changes everything!

For organizations, trust is critical both internally and externally. In fact, given the performance-multiplier effect of high trust, leaders who make building trust a priority are in a position to achieve unprecedented results.

Approximately 160 miles in length, the Wasatch Mountain Range cuts through central Utah. Its numerous peaks, often covered in snow, dominate the landscape and beckon many outdoor enthusiasts. Although many take refuge in the mountains, the vast majority of Utahans live at lower elevations. Provo provides one such example. Overshadowed by Y Mountain, nearly 118,000 people inhabit the growing city with roughly 580,000 in the metro area. Despite the splendor of its surroundings, Provo City government leaders found themselves paying numerous "Trust Taxes." Relationships within departments and among the government, outside agencies, and businesses were strained. Government transparency was lacking, customer service eroded, hiring processes grew lengthier, bureaucracies became more cumbersome, and the organization lacked the ability and willingness to effectively restructure. As if the current challenges weren't enough, the city was not effectively preparing the next generation of city leaders and lacked a culture that would endure changes in elected officials.

We invite you to look around your organization. Do any of these challenges sound familiar?

Provo's mayor, John Curtis, and his leadership team faced the realities of these taxes head on. They discussed the need to transform the organization and change peoples' lives and how they collectively addressed the city's problems. Over the course of a year, Provo City government leaders engaged in the *Speed of Trust Transformation Process.* They worked to create a system of accountability to support long-term, sustainable behavior change. The application of a consistent framework, process, and language allowed Provo City to create new operating norms for daily operations and allowed leaders to reduce much of the inherent friction in their day-to-day work. Everything in Provo started to operate at greater speed and less cost.

Since making the decision to deliberately focus on trust, Provo has been recognized by *Bloomberg* as having the "second-fastest job growth in America,"[69] by *Outside Magazine* as "#2 Greatest Place to Live in America,"[70] and by *Forbes* as "#1 Best Places for Business and Careers."[71]

There's little doubt that every city, every organization would like to see this type of transformation. There's also little doubt that many internal and external factors play a role both in success and failure, but Provo managed to break the cycle of low trust and, in doing so, accomplished amazing results. Mayor Curtis says it best, "There are many things that we would attribute to the success of Provo, but I think in our hearts, we've deeply embedded the culture of the

69. Bloomberg. "Fastest and Slowest Job Growth in America." August 19, 2016. https://www.bloomberg.com/news/articles/2016-08-19/these-are-the-cities-with-the-fastest-and-slowest-job-growth-in-america

70. Outside Magazine Online. "2014 Greatest Places to Live in America." August 12, 2014. https://www.outsideonline.com/1928016/16-best-places-live-us-2014

71. Forbes. "Best Places for Business and Careers." 2014. http://www.forbes.com/pictures/mli45ihgm/1-provo-utah/#4b25392e111f

Speed of Trust principles...speaking a common language as city management has been very powerful."[72]

Inspiring trust and extending trust—these are often the keys to accelerating mission success. And creating such trust is a skill—a performance multiplier—and arguably the key leadership competency needed in today's low-trust environment.

The job used to be...	The job you must do now...
Be one of many government organizations doing good work.	Become the most trusted organization in the government.

How to Build It: The 5 Waves of Trust

But how do you do it? What is the method for building trust?

In *The Speed of Trust*, Stephen M. R. Covey presents a "framework, language, and process" that enables us to establish and grow trust at five levels, or contexts—what he calls "The 5 Waves of Trust." This model derives from the "ripple effect" metaphor that graphically illustrates the interdependent nature of trust and how it flows from the inside out, starting with each of us. It also gives us a framework so

72. Mayor John Curtis. "Speed of Trust Case Study." http://www.speedoftrust.com/video-testimonials-new/provo-city-changing-culture-at-the-speed-of-trust

we can think about trust, a language so we can talk about trust, and a process so we can do something about actually creating trust. The underlying principle behind the first wave, Self Trust, is *credibility*. The key principle behind the second wave, Relationship Trust, is *behavior*. The key principle behind the third wave, Organizational Trust, is *alignment*. The underlying principle of the fourth wave, Market Trust, is *reputation*. And the principle underlying the fifth wave, Societal Trust, is *contribution*. The principles are cumulative as we move from the inside out, creating an exponential effect in growing trust. While the principles are cumulative, the first two principles—credibility and behavior—represent the twin building blocks for how trust is built.

Trust Starts With Who You Are

Where does it start? Ultimately, trust starts with you—with your personal credibility. In *The Speed of Trust,* Covey explains how credibility is the foundation on which all trust is built and how, in the long-run, you'll never have more trust than you have credibility. Credibility is a function of two things: your character (who you are—your integrity and intent), and your competence (what you can do—your capabilities and results). Competence is visible above the surface, while your character, like the roots of a tree, lies beneath the surface and feeds your success—or lack of it.

If we were doing business with you, and you knew that we had all the right professional qualifications and skills but didn't keep our word, you wouldn't trust us and everything would stop. Our lack of character would prevent you from doing business with us, even though we might be the best at what we do. Think of the many high-profile athletes and executives with world-class competence the public no longer trusts because of some very deep lapses in character.

Conversely, if we were doing business with you, and you knew we were honest and cared about you but didn't have the right capabilities, and were no longer relevant and didn't have a track record of results, you also wouldn't trust us and everything would stop. Our lack of competence would undermine the trust, even though we might be extremely honest and caring. You might trust us to watch your home if you went on vacation, but you wouldn't trust us on the key project or deliverable if we didn't have a track record of results.

Both character and competence are vital to building trust, with character being the deeper root, the first among equals. Drilling a level down on the character and competence dimensions enables you to assess yourself against what Covey calls the "4 Cores of Credibility"—the first two cores belonging to character, and the second two belonging to competence.

The first core of credibility is *integrity*. To use the metaphor of the tree, integrity is the root. It means honesty, truthfulness, and congruence. It means doing the right thing. A great educator, Dr. Karl G. Maeser, described in a penetrating way what it means to have integrity: "Place me behind prison walls—walls of stone ever so high, ever so thick, reaching ever so far into the ground—there is a possibility that in some way or another I may escape. But stand me on the floor and draw a chalk line around me and have me give my word of honor never to cross it. Can I get out of the circle? No. Never! I'd die first."[73]

The second core of credibility is *intent*. In our tree metaphor, it's the trunk—part of it is beneath the surface, part of it is above. Intent refers to our motive and agenda. The motive that best builds credibility and trust is when you care about the people you're leading—and they know you care about them. The agenda that best builds credibility and trust is when you are open and seek mutual benefit. That's called win-win. Think about it: when you suspect a hidden agenda from someone, you question everything he or she says and does. Gandhi put it this way: "The moment there is suspicion about a person's motives, everything he does becomes tainted."

---

73. Cited in Ronald J. Burke, et al., *Crime and Corruption in Organizations: Why It Occurs and What to Do About It*, Gower Publishing, 2012, 176.

The motive that best builds credibility and trust is when you care about the people you're leading—and they know you care about them.

The third core of credibility is *capabilities*. On our tree, capabilities are the branches that produce the fruits. Capabilities refer to your ability to inspire confidence, the means you use to produce results. Capabilities comprise your talents, skills, expertise, and knowledge. The key question here is this: Are you relevant? A family doctor might have integrity, his motives might be good, and his track record might be strong, but unless he's trained and skilled to perform a particular task at hand—brain surgery, for example—he'll be lacking in credibility.

The fourth core of credibility is *results*. Results refer to your track record, your performance, your getting the right things done. Results matter enormously to your credibility. People won't and shouldn't trust you if you are unable to "deliver the goods."

Each of these 4 Cores—integrity, intent, capabilities, and results—is vital to personal and organizational credibility, and credibility is the foundation on which all trust is built.

Trust Is Strengthened by How You Act

After credibility, the other key building block to trust is *behavior*. Behavior means what you do—and how you do it. People not only judge your results, they also judge how you achieved them—and how you behave in the marketplace. The astonishing spectacle of high-level business and government leaders pointing fingers and fighting each other during the Great Recession probably destroyed trust as much as anything: "In the midst of the worst economic crisis in decades, people saw their leaders not leading but squabbling and name-calling," complains former San Francisco mayor Gavin Newsom.[74]

It's not enough just to talk about a behavior, you have to put it into action, into practice. Think about trust and your relationships in terms of a bank account—making deposits and withdrawals. Deposits and withdrawals ultimately manifest themselves as behaviors. In *The Speed of Trust*, 13 high-leveraged, trust-creating behaviors are specifically identified. These include keeping commitments, righting wrongs, practicing accountability, demonstrating respect, listening first, and talking straight. The opposite of these 13 Behaviors diminish or even destroy trust: breaking commitments, denying wrongs, shirking responsibility, showing disrespect, failing to listen, and lying.

---

74. Gavin Newsom, *Citizenville: How to Take the Town Square Digital and Reinvent Government*, Penguin Books, 2013, 12.

While the behaviors and their opposites are straightforward and common sense, all too often they are not common practice. The common practice for far too many people and organizations tends to be what are called *Counterfeit Behaviors,* like "spinning" a story—so it is technically true but leaves a false impression—instead of talking straight. Other common Counterfeit Behaviors include covering up a mistake instead of righting the wrong, having hidden agendas instead of creating transparency, blaming others instead of practicing accountability, and overpromising and underdelivering instead of keeping commitments. More often than not, it's the 13 Counterfeit Behaviors, perhaps more than the 13 Opposite Behaviors, that trip up people and organizations, causing them to lose trust. This is because it's fairly obvious the Opposite Behavior will destroy trust (e.g., lying), while the Counterfeit Behavior, like counterfeit money, is deceptive in that it appears to work but ultimately diminishes trust (e.g., spinning).

Building Trust at Frito-Lay

While studying and applying Stephen M. R. Covey's work on *The Speed of Trust*, the executives of Frito-Lay became fascinated with the idea that building trust could speed things up and lower costs. "Frito-Lay was never a low-trust company," Covey says, but CEO Al Carey wanted to reignite the corporate culture. Like all good leaders, he wanted things to be cheaper, faster, and better, but he also wanted to energize people, to help them "lean into" their work—in short, to reengage them.

Hundreds of bureaucratic rules and procedures were swept away. Layers of decision making were removed. The administrative changes were fueled by the introspective work people did on themselves as they learned a method for building trust.

"We didn't just teach skills—we changed the culture," says Cheryl Cerminara, a vice president at Frito-Lay. "Pick two people: One you trust in both competency and character. The other you expect to flub up and/or stab you in the back. Then think about the extra work, energy, and frustration the untrustworthy person causes. Low trust is exhausting and stressful. You hear people say, 'I have to send a million follow-up emails.' 'I worry about it all the way home.' 'It upsets my work/life balance.' Everybody has been in a situation like this. It becomes much harder not to act with integrity when everyone around you is."[75]

The method cascaded through the organization and transformed Frito-Lay. For the first time they critiqued their untrustworthy behaviors. They held regular "Trust Talks" at every level, identifying and winnowing out problems.

---

75. Cheryl Hall, "Frito-Lay Puts Trust in Trust," *Dallas Morning News*, Mar. 9, 2011. http://www.dallasnews.com/business/columnists/cheryl-hall/20110308-frito-lay-puts-trust-in-trust.ece

They held checkpoint meetings quarterly to evaluate their progress in becoming a more trusted company. "We learned to trust each other," says Al Carey. "So there was no need for the extra bureaucracy."

In 2008, the company faced gigantic challenges: a sudden spike in fuel prices and the worst economic collapse in 70 years. Then the cost of their raw material—potatoes—went up tenfold because heavy rains spoiled the crops. Financial disaster threatened. But Frito-Lay was ready with a new perspective and a new skillset: with their highly accelerated decision-making processes, they navigated through the threat. The entire pricing system was reengineered in five weeks instead of the sixteen weeks it normally took. "What would normally take us two months of wrangling, we did in ten days."

Instead of suffering financial disaster, Frito-Lay shot past expectations and produced one of its best years ever. "It was the best profit growth we'd had in ten years," Al Carey says. "I credit *The Speed of Trust*. We moved through decisions that are enormously complex at breakneck speed. We made five sets of tough decisions throughout the whole year, and we never before would have been able to make those decisions as quickly as we did.... It's the most exciting culture change I've seen in my twenty-eight years with the company."[76]

As a leader, your influence counts. By building up your own credibility and then behaving in ways that establish trust, you'll go a long way toward inspiring High-Trust Behavior transformations in others.

Building Trust: Instructions for Downloading

Here's how to build trust with others[77]:

Step	Checkpoints
1. The 4 Cores of Credibility: Assess Your Character	**Integrity** How do you view your own actions? Are they aligned with your own deepest values?
	Intent What's your agenda? Is it hidden or out in the open?
2. The 4 Cores of Credibility: Assess Your Competence	**Capabilities** Can you deliver what you promise? Are you still relevant?
	Results What's your track record?

76. "Al Carey, CEO of Frito-Lay, on *The Speed of Trust*," YouTube, n.d. http://www.youtube.com/watch?v=JZqK3MKxbpo

77. See Stephen M. R. Covey, *The Speed of Trust: The One Thing That Changes Everything*, Free Press, 2006.

Step	Checkpoints
3. Practice 13 Trust Behaviors	1. Talk Straight. Are you honest? Do you tell the truth? 2. Demonstrate Respect. Do you genuinely care about the people around you? 3. Create Transparency. Do you tell the truth in a way people can verify for themselves? 4. Right Wrongs. Do you apologize quickly? Do you make restitution where possible? 5. Show Loyalty. Do you give credit to others? Do you bad-mouth people behind their back? 6. Deliver Results. Do you get the right things done? 7. Get Better. Are you a constant learner? 8. Confront Reality. Do you address the tough stuff directly? 9. Clarify Expectations. Do you write them down? Do you discuss them? Do you violate them? 10. Practice Accountability. Do you take responsibility for results, good and bad? 11. Listen First. Do you assume that you know what others think and feel without listening? 12. Keep Commitments. Do you attempt to spin your way out of a commitment you've broken? 13. Extend Trust. Do you trust others based on the situation, the risk, and credibility of the people involved, but err on the side of trust?

CHAPTER 9

PRACTICE 5: CREATE INTENSE LOYALTY

HOW TO STAY TRUE TO THOSE YOU SERVE

–

"You can buy a person's hand, but you can't buy his heart. His heart is where his enthusiasm, his loyalty is."
–Stephen R. Covey

–

Every ninety days, more than two billion people visit U.S. government websites. They come seeking information about the weather (weather.gov), taxes (irs.gov), postal service (usps.gov), and a wide range of assistance, support, and other valuable information. The complexity of sites and sheer volume of information can quickly overwhelm users. Fortunately, one leader, Martha Dorris, and her team at the General Services Administration (GSA) Office of Citizen Services, has created a customer-centric means for helping customers navigate the government's Web presence.

Dorris and her team designed, developed, and currently maintain a powerful search engine, an extensive social-media presence, multiple crowdsourcing tools, and a network of Web portals all focused on one thing—making the customer experience as easy as possible. "The way people are going to expect government services is changing and we have to change with it," said Dan Tangherlini, the acting administrator of GSA, "Martha is helping citizens connect directly with the services they need. When they write the history for that change, she will be one of the founding people." Dave McClure, associate GSA administrator for the Office of Citizen Services and Innovative Technologies, adds, "Martha is almost the citizens' ombudsman for positive and fruitful interactions with government."[78]

We invite you to think about the last time you came to the government for services. You didn't come in any official capacity; you simply came as a private citizen, a customer. Perhaps you were looking to renew a driver's license, file a building permit, request Social Security benefits, or a myriad of services the government—at all levels—provides. What was your experience like? What did you walk away thinking or feeling? What did your customer experience convey to you about the individual who served you and the broader government organization?

78. Partnership for Public Service (PPS), Samual J. Heyman Service to America Medals 2013 Finalist – Citizen Services. https://servicetoamericamedals.org/honorees/view_profile.php?profile=340

If you are a U.S. resident, there's a good chance your experience was less than satisfactory. The American Customer Satisfaction Index (ACSI)[79] reports that in 2015, customer satisfaction fell for the third year in a row to a 63.9 on a 100-point scale. *Public Manager Magazine* contends that "American citizens are generally not satisfied with their interaction with federal services. When asked what they like or dislike about dealing with government, respondents cited less-than-courteous and unprofessional behavior by staff. In fact, assessments of these indicators plunged 5 percent, compared with one year ago."[80]

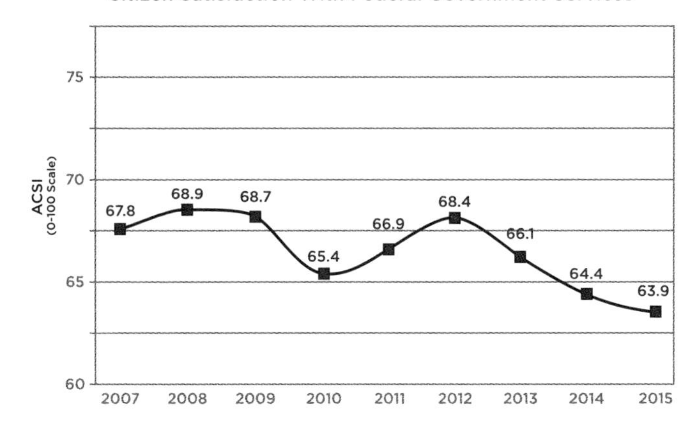

79. American Customer Service Index. "ACSI Federal Government Report 2015" http://www.theacsi.org/news-and-resources/customer-satisfaction-reports/reports-2015/acsi-federal-government-report-2015

80. *The Public Manager Magazine*, "What Will Bad Customer Service Cost Government?" June 15, 2015.

Probably the highest level of engagement is *loyalty*. Loyal workers and loyal customers are worth gold. A talented worker who gives her heart and mind to your enterprise can generate significantly better results and good will than she will ever cost you and the organization. A customer who gives you a lifetime of loyalty and word-of-mouth support is *the* ultimate mission-essential lever.

In business, the old paradigm was "customer and employee satisfaction" and companies put programs and efforts in place to create that satisfaction. The same is true for many government organizations. Post offices, departments of motor vehicles, state and national parks, and a myriad of other customer-facing government organizations have, to varying degrees, worked to achieve customer and employee satisfaction. Admittedly, there have been many government organizations that have yet to embrace a satisfaction mindset. These organizations appear to behave as if they have a monopoly on the services they provide, and "those" people (not their customers or those they serve) have to comply with what the government wants, not the other way around. If your organization has this mindset, we remind you to revisit the story of Sandy Spring, Georgia, and consider the reality that no organization, not even yours, has the inherent right to exist.

Moreover, government organizations need to move away from the mindset of having "satisfied" customers and employees. That's just not enough anymore. The new paradigm is "intense loyalty," and shifting to that paradigm is the job you must do *now*.

"Satisfaction"—The Old Paradigm

Most customer-satisfaction surveys don't lead to meaningful change. The surveys are often poorly designed, too long, and biased. The questions are frequently crafted to get certain answers, which makes the resulting data inaccurate. Many of the questions are centered less on customer issues and more on "how did we do?"

Obviously, the quality of leadership is, at bottom, the reason for loyalty or disloyalty among employees and customers. Reliance on pro forma "satisfaction" scores is lazy, twentieth-century thinking and a formula for complacency; the real question for leaders is, "How do you build intense loyalty?"

Reliance on pro forma "satisfaction" scores is lazy, twentieth-century thinking and a formula for complacency

The job used to be...	The job you must do now...
Satisfy internal and external customers.	Create intense loyalty.

"Intense Loyalty"—The New Paradigm

How do you get the kind of intense engagement that was so movingly demonstrated by the workforce at the Transport for London's (TfL) Bakerloo Line? How do you create customer-aligned solutions like those championed by Martha Dorris and her team?

The answer, according to Harvard professor and veteran Bain consultant Dr. Fred Reichheld, is "to treat them the way you would want to be treated." This principle, known as the Golden Rule, is laughably simple—and it works. Reichheld cites Colleen Barrett, president of wildly successful Southwest Airlines: "Practicing the Golden Rule is integral to everything we do." And Andy Taylor of Enterprise, the most prosperous rental-car company in the world: "The only way to grow is to treat customers so well they come back for more and tell their friends about us."[81]

81. Fred Reichheld, *The Ultimate Question*, Harvard Business School Publishing, 2006, 14.

"Practicing the Golden Rule is integral to everything we do."
— Southwest Airlines

A friend of ours on a business trip got stranded in a small town in the American Midwest. His flight was canceled, it was long past closing time for the only rental-car office at the tiny airport, but he thought he'd try the door. A smiling young man in a white shirt and tie opened it. He was an Enterprise employee, who quickly signed out the last rental car in town to our friend.

"Why are you even here?" our friend asked. "It's awfully late."

The young man answered, "I heard the flight out of town got canceled, so I figured somebody would probably need me." Then he pulled a cake out of his small refrigerator. "My wife made this cake today and brought it over for anybody who might want some. Would you like a piece?" Our friend had missed his dinner and actually was kind of hungry. He thankfully took it on a plate with a fork and a napkin, and it was delicious.

Then the young man said, "Here, take the whole cake. You've got a long drive to Des Moines."

Our friend, who had never done business with Enterprise before, is now a lifetime customer. "They take the cake!" he says. Enterprise systematically instills the Golden Rule into every one of its nearly 70,000 employees, and as a result is named year after year the most customer-friendly car-rental company.

An "Intense Loyalty" App

Government organizations need a *system*—an "application"—for building loyalty all along the journey of the client or employee. For a long time, leaders have focused on improving "moments of truth"—touchpoints where customers might come in contact with the firm. This is helpful, but it produces excellence only in spots. Researchers say, "Organizations able to skillfully manage the entire experience reap enormous rewards: enhanced customer satisfaction, reduced churn, increased revenue, and greater employee satisfaction too."[82]

A loyalty "app" starts with both customer- and employee-loyalty measures. Many organizations are now using Reichheld's well-regarded "Net Promoter Score" as their key measure of both: It's the ratio between people who would recommend your organization as a great place to work or

82. Alex Rawson, et al. "The Truth About the Customer Experience," *Harvard Business Review*, Sep. 2013. http://hbr.org/2013/09/the-truth-about-customer-experience/ar/1

do business and those who definitely would not. If your score is 100, everyone recommends you; if it's -100, nobody does. A score of 50 or more is unusually high because you have many more "promoters" than "detractors."

The Net Promoter Score provides a credible baseline measurement of loyalty, but you need other information to tell you what to *do* about your score. That information comes from careful analysis of customer input—in other words, Empathic Listening. What is the customer or employee telling you specifically about yourself? What things do they specify when praising you or complaining about you? From this analytical work, you can isolate the lead measures to work on. Leaders who combine a true measure of loyalty like the Net Promoter Score with a rich system of input are most likely to know what to do to move that score in the right direction. Once you know the score, you can make leaps in loyalty a Wildly Important Goal—and you should.

Powerful Lead Measures: Fascinated People

Some organizations have powerful lead measures, behaviors that are predictive of goal achievement and influenceable by the team, for driving loyalty among all stakeholders. One unique organization is Grupo Entero of Guatemala City, a diverse and thriving enterprise providing services that often intersect with those provided by many government organizations, started by Juan Mauricio Bonifasi, known as "Juanma." A careful student of the 7 Habits for some years, Juanma conceived of an organization that would be based on the principles of the 7 Habits, an organization where proactive, visionary people could flourish. Juanma doesn't distinguish between clients and employees—they are all *colaboradores*, or contributors.

"Our primary goal," he says, "is to fascinate our contributors, to create a culture where people are fulfilled by using their talents in passions in their work."

> **"Our primary goal is to fascinate our contributors, to create a culture where people are fulfilled by using their talents in passions in their work."**
> **—Grupo Entero**

Grupo Entero is essentially a holding entity, a nursery for entrepreneurial efforts staffed with *fascinados*—"fascinated people." One branch of the organization is Guateprenda, a microcredit bank that lends money to low-income borrowers who want to start their own businesses. No traditional bank would lend to such people. But just a small loan can make a huge difference to a farmer who needs a truck for his market garden or a single mother who could make a lot more money selling snow cones if she had more equipment and a storefront. Guateprenda's people become emotional when they talk about the tremendous difference they are making throughout Central America. Another Grupo Entero undertaking is Sonríe, a chain of dental clinics "dedicated to freeing people from pain and helping them maximize their potential." The staffers at Sonríe work miracles for suffering children and disfigured adults who gain new confidence in the workplace.

We're enthralled by Juanma's notion that each individual associated with his Grupo Entero, whether client or employee, is considered a "contributor," a *fascinado* who is finding an outlet for his or her passion and potential. What a remarkable business model—a company that exists not just to make money, although Grupo Entero thrives financially as people clamor to be part of an enterprise dedicated to unleashing the potential of every contributor. He and his fellow leaders invest heavily in both time and money to understand and develop that potential so it can be leveraged. Every contributor is thoroughly trained in the *7 Habits*, the "mental operating system" of the company, and then a development plan is tailored carefully—a plan that will leverage the individual's "fascination" in life. It's the whole purpose of Grupo Entero to see those dreams realized.

A Loss of Productivity: Passionless People

Contrast Grupo Entero with the development practices of most organizations. "It's hard to think of an important aspect of management more neglected than development planning: helping employees shape the future direction of their careers," says business executive and writer Victor Lipman. "Yet, this valuable activity is ignored or handled as a bureaucratic exercise or an afterthought.

"People care if you take a genuine interest in their future. Taking an honest interest in someone builds loyalty. Loyal employees are more engaged. Engaged employees are more productive."[83]

"People care if you take a genuine interest in their future. Taking an honest interest in someone builds loyalty."
—Victor Lipman

Employee Loyalty Leads to Customer Loyalty

It's also fascinating to note how employee loyalty affects customer loyalty, which in turn affects mission

83. Victor Lipman, "Why Employee Development Is Important but Neglected," *Psychology Today*, Mar. 13, 2013. http://www.psychologytoday.com/blog/mind-the-manager/201303/why-employee-development-is-important-neglected

accomplishment. As noted in our opening chapter, the government environment has become intensely pressurized. Media scrutiny, calls for transparency, shrinking budgets, and other such factors have placed tremendous pressure on government leaders and employees. Couple these challenges with the nature of the work many organizations face. As ACSI chairman and founder, Claes Fornell, explains, "Due to the very nature of their business, regulatory agencies like the IRS always face user-satisfaction challenges. These problems are exacerbated by inconsistent and ineffective leadership practices (see Chapter 3). To some degree, it's not surprising that customer satisfaction continues to plummet; what's concerning is if organizations merely accept this as the status quo and continue down the same poor customer-service path. We are reminded of what Rear Admiral Grace Hopper said over 50 years ago, "the most dangerous phrase in the language is we've always done it that way."

By contrast, organizations that work to gain the intense loyalty of their employees tend also to gain the intense loyalty of their customers. Grupo Entero embodies this principle with its philosophy of cultivating loyal contributors. USA.gov harnesses the power of loyalty through unleashing the innovation of its employees and customers. While bureaucracies are historically known for command and control, stagnation, and unneeded complexity, Martha Dorris and her team look to tap into everyone's contribution through their Challenge.gov efforts. "It is a way to unearth innovation and new thinking from people," explains Dorris.

Moving the Middle

As far as we know, no organization has ever earned a Net Promoter Score of 100. Getting into the 70s puts you among an elite organization, while the average score is between 10 and 15.[84] If you're a leader, one of your Wildly Important Goals is to raise that score, whatever it is, because of the critical value of stakeholder loyalty. A realistic strategy for doing that is to "move the middle," whether you're leading a small team or an entire organization.

Every business has promoters and detractors. Some promoters (like your mother) will love you, no matter what you do. Some detractors (hopefully, not your mother) will hate you, no matter what you do. You're not likely to affect the feelings of people at either end of the spectrum, but in the middle is the vast majority who could be influenced. If you can move that group even a few points toward the promoter spectrum, you reap huge dividends because the group is so large.

84. John Warrilow, "One Question Can Predict the Future of Your Company," *Inc.*, Jun. 24, 2011. http://www.inc.com/articles/201106/whats-your-net-promoter-score.html

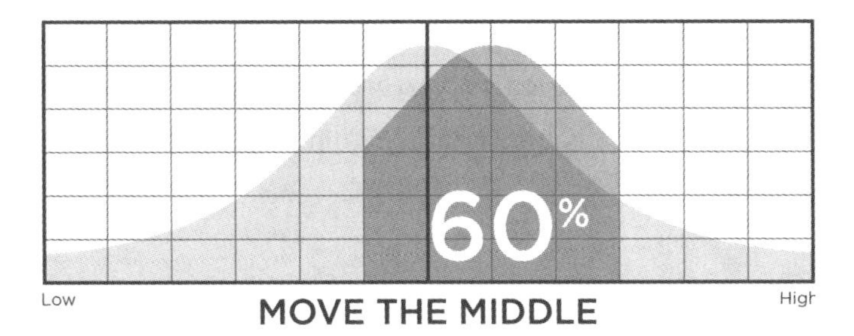

Anything you can do to move the middle toward intense loyalty will reap big benefits. Often passive customers can become very loyal customers if you listen with empathy to their issues. For example, Shawn says, “I’m very happy with my tablet. I love it. I’m a ‘middling’ user—I enjoy getting Wi-Fi access to my favorite social-media and news sites and an occasional movie, but I’m neither a techie early adopter nor a cranky old Luddite. I’m just loyal to my tablet.

“But if I were asked, I do have a few issues with it. I’d like to have a protective case that isn’t so heavy. I get knocked off my applications too often. I know I have to sync it, but I wish I didn’t. The app store is hard for me to navigate. And sometimes the connection problems make me want to throw it out the window.

Often passive customers can become very loyal customers if you listen with empathy to their issues.

"I recognize my issues are petty and unreasonable, but tablet-computer designers who are also empathic listeners might be able to help. And if they did, my loyalty to their product would zoom up into the fervency zone."

The Intensity Zone

Because the rewards of intense loyalty are so great, you should be gripped by the goal of achieving the "intensity zone," where people wouldn't want to work with anyone but you. Who can calculate the value of workers who will wade through the mud for each other and their organization? Or the value of customers who feel almost religiously tied to you? Moving the most people possible toward the fervency zone should be a Wildly Important Goal for every leader, and the job you must do now.

Creating Intense Loyalty: Instructions for Downloading

Step	Discussion Points
5. Measure your customer and employee loyalty.	• One way to do this is to calculate the Net Promoter Score. • Ask this question: "On a scale from 0 to 10 (with 10 being high), how likely is it that you would recommend us to a friend or colleague? Please give your reasons for your answer."

Categorize the scores as follows:

Score	Category
9-10	Promoters: Loyal, enthusiastic, will give you return business and refer others.
7-8	Passives: Satisfied but not enthusiastic, vulnerable to competitors.
0-6	Detractors: Unhappy, will give you negative word of mouth.
To calculate the Net Promoter Score, subtract the percentage who are detractors from the percentage who are promoters.	

6. Set a goal to improve your loyalty measure.	• Set a Wildly Important Goal to improve the Net Promoter Score. Choose a number you think is attainable and give yourself a deadline to achieve it.
7. Act on your lead measures.	• Analyze carefully the reasons the respondents gave for their choices. Look for recurring themes. • Drill deeper into those recurring themes. Get on the phone and the social media, go talk to customers and employees face-to-face. Get to the bottom of the issues people are raising about you. • As a team, select lead measures based on the themes you've discovered. • Act on the lead measures and carefully track your progress.

CONCLUSION: THE JOB FOR YOU TO DO NOW STARTS TODAY

START NOW AND MOVE THE NEEDLE IN THE RIGHT DIRECTION

-

"A blank page is no empty space. It is brimming with potential. It is a masterpiece in waiting—yours."

–A. A. Patawaran

-

In this book, we've seen how your people—the ultimate source of mission accomplishment—can become highly effective leaders at every level of the organization, can create engagement by connecting to the "voice of the organization, can execute with excellence, can contribute infinitely more than they imagined, can become the most trusted in the government, and can create fervent loyalty both internal to the organization and within the broader environment. A culture that puts these practices in place is what a highly effective organization looks like, and that's the kind of organization you need to create now.

In the past, it was probably enough to be a good manager, figuring out how to do more with less, "adding value," making sure your customers and employees were satisfied. But no more. It's time to move beyond the mindset that every team member's role, and yours, should be prescribed and you all subscribe to it. That way of thinking doesn't ask much of our heart or brain. It's more of a clock-in/clock-out mentality: insert your job description into your head in the morning and eject it in the evening. Under that system, the job to be done is programmed for you.

That system had its place, but now our lives are far more exacting—and also more fascinating. Everyone can be a leader. In fact, individual leadership is an imperative! The way is open for people to make an infinitely more significant contribution than they ever imagined they could. In addition to your organization's unique mission, your mission as a leader is to achieve your own great purpose by helping others achieve theirs. The maxim now is *meaning*.

Your mission as a leader is to achieve your own great purpose by helping others achieve theirs. The maxim now is meaning.

The leader's job has changed fundamentally. The mental operating system is no longer "control" but "unleash." It's founded in purpose and principles instead of compliance and calculation. Dee Hock, the innovative leader who created the Visa card, describes this mindset: "To the degree that you hold purpose and principles in common among you, you can dispense with command and control. People will know how to behave in accordance with them, and they'll do it in thousands of unimaginable, creative ways. The organization will become a vital, living set of beliefs."

Too much of the old mindset persists. Until we choose to be empathic, we'll continue to lead from an inner core of indifference, but people know instinctively when they're being stage-managed. "Leaders are often tossed and turned," Dr. Covey said. "Should they be more democratic or more autocratic? Firmer or more permissive? Tell more or ask more? What are the best techniques for getting things done through people? These questions are important and must be considered, but they are secondary questions. The primary question is: How much do you really care?"

Do you care enough to do what is required?

To make the choice to be a *leader*, not just a job description?

To help others become leaders—to install an operating system that enables leaders at all levels?

To unleash people to contribute infinitely more than you imagined they could?

To execute your most important goals with excellence and precision?

To become the most trusted of leaders?

To help your customers succeed in their own great purposes?

To create intense loyalty among the people you serve?

These are the tough but exhilarating choices leaders have to make now. In this book, we have walked through the principles, the paradigms, and the practices of this new kind of leadership; if you make good use of them, you'll be equal to the challenge of becoming a true leader.

But what if you don't *feel* equal to the challenge? What if you're afraid to make that choice because of the weight of organizational politics? "What will they say if I suddenly become proactive and visionary and empathic? How will they react if I start saying no to things that don't matter much so I can say yes to things that do? What will happen if I question a strategy or policy that won't help the client succeed? Will they even *let* me be a leader?"

Whoever "they" are, don't worry about them.

More than a century ago, researchers at Clark University did an experiment with a walleye pike, a very aggressive fish. The researchers placed the pike in a large tank filled with water and added several minnows, the pike's natural food, and watched as the fish immediately devoured the minnows. The researchers then placed a transparent glass divider in the tank with new minnows on one side and the pike on the other. Again, the larger fish went after the minnows, this time hitting its head against the glass with each attempt. Eventually, the pike stopped trying to eat the minnows, having learned that the effort would only bring a sore head.

After three months, the researchers removed the glass barrier. Now there was nothing separating the predator from its prey. Yet, even with the minnows now swimming all around the tank, the pike made no attempt to eat them. The pike would starve to death before trying to eat its favorite meal.[85] Such is the power of discouragement (or a sore head!). We may have tried and failed in the past, and because we learned that trying can occasionally bring failure and pain, we assume it will always be so.

Don't believe it.

---

85. "Scientific Fish Story," *The New York Times,* Aug. 25, 1901. http://query.nytimes.com/mem/archive-free/pdf?res=F60811F83F5B11738DDDAC0A94D0405B818CF1D3

When you focus your energy on things you can't control, your influence shrinks. You may still be worried about politics—about your position with this or that person or who's getting pro-/demoted or who's up, down, or sideways. But this is debilitating thinking that will only diminish your capacity to contribute. By contrast, if you choose to focus your energy on the things you *can* do something about, your influence grows—often dramatically. You can't control what others do; you can only hope to *influence* them. You contribute what you can instead of exhausting your energy in futile political games, because your allegiance is to the principles, not to the players.

If you choose to focus your energy on the things you can do something about, your influence grows—often dramatically.

You will make mistakes: All leaders do. You may feel awkward at first, but if you persist, you will eventually feel the excitement of real growth in yourself, your team, and the bottom line.

This book begins with two stories: the heroic account of a highly engaged team in London's Bakerloo Line, and the story of a guy named Tom who had stopped contributing. His body was going to work, but his mind and heart were elsewhere. He had allowed an autocratic system, void of vision or purpose, to siphon away his passion and energy.

You don't have to be Tom. You can choose to be a proactive leader and bring vision and purpose to your work. You can be the leader of a team every bit as engaged as the people who keep the Bakerloo Line trains running.

Rosabeth Moss Kanter says, "A vision is not just a picture of what could be; it is an appeal to our better selves, a call to become something more." So, what is your picture of what could be? What is your "something more"?

Let's get started...

ABOUT THE AUTHORS

Patrick Leddin, Ph.D.
Senior Consultant, FranklinCovey Associate
Professor, Vanderbilt

Patrick is an associate professor of Management Studies at Vanderbilt University and a senior consultant at FranklinCovey. He is an expert in the areas of strategy creation and execution, leader development, and organizational culture. He has worked with private and public sector clients in the United States, Canada, Asia, the Caribbean, and throughout Europe. Patrick has more than 25-years of leadership and project-management experience. He began his career as an officer in the United States Army, where he completed a number of the military's most challenging leadership-development courses including airborne, ranger, and infantry officer schools, and he held leadership positions such as infantry platoon leader and company commander in the 82nd Airborne Division. While working for a Big Five consulting firm, he led project teams to design, develop, and implement project deliverables that exactly met client needs. He is the author of *Oliver's Spot: The Five Ps Leading Teams to Top Results and Oliver's Spot for the Public Sector: A Leadership Story*.

Shawn D. Moon
Former Executive Vice President, Strategic Markets
FranklinCovey

Shawn is the former Executive Vice President of Leadership and Strategic Accounts at FranklinCovey, which included responsibility for the company's Government Services division. For over thirty years, he has worked with clients across the globe, from Fortune 500 to governmental organizations, bringing his first-hand experience in leadership and management, sales and marketing, program development, and consulting services in both the private and public sectors.

Shawn is the author or co-author of several books, including *Fierce Loyalty: Earning the Love of Customers and Employees to Power Growth, Talent Unleashed: 3 Leadership Conversations to Ignite the Unlimited Potential in People,* as well as *The Ultimate Competitive Advantage: Why Your People Make All the Difference and 6 Practices You Need to Engage Them.*

ACKNOWLEDGMENTS

A project like this is only successful because of the tireless efforts of so many people. We first express our most sincere gratitude to the remarkable clients we've been able to work with and serve for many years. Their leadership and commitment to building winning cultures—all with the end goal of accomplishing the significant and inspiring missions they were established to serve—is deeply inspiring. Our clients' willingness to work, change, challenge, and to partner has provided new insights and direction. Their experiences have contributed greatly to our work and many of their stories are found in this book.

We acknowledge the ongoing contributions of our colleagues, including senior consultants, practice leaders, client partners, administrative partners, and the FranklinCovey executive team. Their support and ongoing work, on the ground and with our clients, brings great thought leadership to the task of achieving results in the public sectors.

Special thanks go to Rylee O'Dowd, Annie Oswald, Jody Karr, and the Creative Lab at FranklinCovey, without whose efforts this book would never have happened.

Preston Luke has been an integral part of this project from the beginning. His leadership and vision with the Government

Services team has powerfully impacted FranklinCovey's work across all sectors of Government.

Our personal and professional lives have forever been shaped by our association with the late Dr. Stephen R. Covey. His contributions continue to roll across and impact the world.

Finally, we thank our families. Stephen R. Covey once defined leadership as "communicating to people their worth and potential so clearly that they come to see it in themselves." Thank you for your willingness to see, communicate, and encourage what we often couldn't see in ourselves. Your love and unflagging support is the reason any of this has happened.

THE ULTIMATE COMPETITIVE ADVANTAGE

FranklinCovey is a global company specializing in performance improvement. We help organizations achieve results that require a change in human behavior.

Our expertise is in seven areas:

LEADERSHIP

Develops highly effective leaders who engage others to achieve results.

EXECUTION

Enables organizations to execute strategies that require a change in human behavior.

PRODUCTIVITY

Equips people to make high-value choices and execute with excellence in the midst of competing priorities.

TRUST

Builds a high-trust culture of collaboration and engagement, resulting in greater speed and lower costs.

SALES PERFORMANCE

Transforms the buyer-seller relationship by helping clients succeed.

CUSTOMER LOYALTY

Drives faster growth and improves frontline performance with accurate customer- and employee-loyalty data.

EDUCATION

Helps schools transform their performance by unleashing the greatness in every educator and student.

OTHER BOOKS FROM FRANKLINCOVEY

The 7 Habits of Highly Effective People

The 8th Habit

The 3rd Alternative

Primary Greatness

First Things First

Principle-Centered Leadership

The Leader in Me

Great Work Great Career

Predictable Results in Unpredictable Times

The 4 Disciplines of Execution

Project Management for the Unofficial Project Manager

Presentation Advantage

The Ultimate Competitive Advantage

Talent Unleashed

Get Better